W9-AEV-447

Partners In Purpose And Progress:

A Brief History

Of The Education Commission

Of The Southern Baptist Convention

by

H. I. Hester

ii

INTRODUCTION

In 1968 Dr. Hester wrote *Southern Baptists in Christian Education.* Using this book as a foundation, he has covered a significant period in the development and growth of Southern Baptist colleges and schools.

There is no better qualified person in the Southern Baptist Convention to perform such a task. Dr. Hester is himself a graduate of Wake Forest University and of the Southern Baptist Theological Seminary. He began his classroom career as a teacher at Furman University and later went to William Jewell College, where he served as head of the Bible department from 1926 to 1961. He became the first chairman of the board of trustees of Midwestern Baptist Theological Seminary, and served as vice-president of that institution from 1961 to 1965.

Dr. Hester is a well-known scholar, having produced countless articles and monographs, as well as several books of history and Biblical studies. He is best known for *The Heart of Hebrew History* (Old Testament history) and *The Heart of the New Testament.* These books have gone through seventy printings.

He has served as secretary-treasurer of the Association of Southern Baptist Colleges and Schools since 1948, and has worked with the Education Commission since 1936.

In 1972, Dr. and Mrs. H. I. Hester endowed through the Southern Baptist Foundation the Hester Lecture Series, which has already enabled the Association of Southern Baptist Colleges and Schools to secure for the annual program the services of several outstanding and nationally known speakers.

Dr. Hester's easy, flowing style comes from his personal knowledge of people and events for more than fifty years. He has served the Commission and Association without pay, and this updated history is also a work of love. It is a pleasure to commend this book to all those who are interested in a contemporary historical narrative of Southern Baptist educational institutions.

Ben C. Fisher
Executive Director-Treasurer
Education Commission of the
Southern Baptist Convention

Nashville, Tennessee
October, 1977

AUTHOR'S FOREWORD

...st Convention is so vast and so complex that comparatively few of our number can claim a satisfactory knowledge of the whole field of operations.

The leaders in the field of Southern Baptist higher education, like the leaders of the other agencies of the Convention, must seek constantly to inform the people of what has been done and is being done in the area of higher education. The Convention agency responsible for the work of our schools and colleges is the Education Commission. For more than 60 years the commission has served faithfully. It has made a magnificent contribution which has been too often overlooked. "If only the people knew, what a difference it would make."

The purpose of this little volume is to give some of the highlights in the remarkable story of higher education among Southern Baptists in the last half century. It is the hope of the author that the book may serve that purpose.

H. I. Hester

Liberty, Missouri
October, 1977

v

CONTENTS

vii

CHAPTER I

Since the matter with which we shall deal in this little volume is an essential part of the work of the Southern Baptist Convention, it will be well to look briefly at this large body of Christian people in the United States. While this denomination originated in the South and for many years was found only south of the Mason and Dixon line, today Southern Baptists are to be found in all the states of the union. Indeed, one may find some of them in most of the countries of the world.

This denomination was officially organized "in the meeting house of the Baptist Church in Augusta, Georgia," May, 1845. Delegates had assembled from several states "pursuant to a call by the board of managers of the Virginia Foreign Mission Society." One record, which presumably is correct, states that there were 236 delegates (messengers) from 165 churches.

The preamble to the constitution of the general convention states clearly the purpose of this assembly: "3, the delegates of the Missionary Societies, Churches, and other religious bodies of the Baptist Denomination, in various parts of the United States, met in

Convention . . . for the purpose of carrying into effect the benevolent intentions of our constituents, for organizing a plan for eliciting, combining and directing the energies of the whole denomination in one sacred effort, for the propagation of the Gospel." The only "boards" or official agencies of the group at the start were the Foreign Mission Board and the Home Mission Board. As we shall see, other boards and commissions were added as time passed.

In the year of its founding the record shows that in this new convention there were 4,126 churches with 351,951 members. Ten years later there were 6,590 churches with a membership of 542,396.

In 1895, fifty years after its origin, the Southern Baptist Convention had a membership of 1,468,991 people in 18,143 local congregations. When one considers the terrible disruption and poverty brought by the Civil War and the period of reconstruction, he has to marvel at the great progress made by these zealous Christian people. However, as we shall see, the greatest period of growth and development has come in the last four decades.

We may be able to understand the remarkable growth and achievements of Southern Baptists by looking briefly at their distinguishing characteristics. The great majority of their members have been English-speaking people. For the most part they have lived in rural areas and in villages and small towns. For many years most of them were farmers. Their rural churches were at the center of their living and thinking. While there were always some well-educated people in their churches, most of their members, like their neighbors, were not highly educated.

Through the years Southern Baptists have been conservative in their living and in their religious beliefs. This characteristic varies from place to place, but as a rule they hold to the generally accepted doctrines of evangelical Christians. Perhaps their best known distinction is their loyalty to the Bible as the inspired word of God.

As we have already noted, the chief motive leading to their organization as a denomination was their concern for missions. While their record in foreign missions has not been ideal, it is still true that they have far surpassed many other denominations in these endeavors. Indeed, thoughtful observers declare that the one great factor which has united and inspired Southern Baptists is their devotion to the missionary enterprises.

One other distinction belonging to Southern Baptists is their belief in evangelism. They have never surrendered their conviction that all men are sinners, and that all men can be saved only by personal faith in Jesus Christ. In this experience a man is "born again" and is then a citizen of the Kingdom of God. In early years some evangelistic work was done through "camp meetings." The practice of conducting "revival meetings" in local churches has been

side the "original territory" of the Convention. This expansion began gradually as people living in the South moved into other states. Many of these wanted the kind of church life in their new home to which they had become accustomed. Of course, some of these newcomers became members of churches they found in their new communities; some never united with any church; but some yearned for church life such as they had enjoyed at home. It was these who led in establishing Southern Baptist churches in their new homes. In all these states there were many people who had no church affiliation, and this fact offered a great challenge for personal work. The results of these labors, especially in the Midwestern and Western states, have been most encouraging. Thus in more than one hundred years of their history Southern Baptists have become the largest non-Catholic body of Christians in the United States.

The growth of Southern Baptists has not been in numbers only. With the passing of time and as conditions changed, they have enlarged the number of Convention agencies and have developed new plans of operation. We have seen that the only official agencies at first were the Foreign Mission Board and the Home Mission Board.

Before the beginning of the twentieth century there was a strong demand for an agency to foster and encourage the teaching of the Bible, and to provide other literature for teaching people. Consequently, on May 26, 1891, the Baptist Sunday School Board was organized in Nashville, Tennessee. Most of the Baptist people themselves would be amazed at the phenomenal growth of this agency and the extent of its varied ministries today.

Early in this century there had developed an urgent demand for some agency whose responsibility would be to provide economic security for the pastor in old age. The response to this need culminated in the establishing of the Relief and Annuity Board (now called the Annuity Board) in 1918, with headquarters in Fort Worth, Texas. Its program has now been greatly expanded to include various other denominational workers.

As Baptist schools and colleges grew in number and influence, leaders in the Convention felt that these should be recognized and assisted by the Convention. At its meeting in Houston, Texas, in 1915 the Convention authorized the establishing of the Education Commission. The full story of the work of this important commission will be told in the remaining chapters of this book.

As the vast potential of radio (and later television) began to be grasped, the possibility of its use by the Convention became a live issue. At the meeting of the Convention in Richmond in 1938 Dr. Samuel Franklin Lowe petitioned the body to "explore this field of radio broadcasting as a possible medium of projecting the Baptist message." Dr. Lowe was named chairman of a committee of seven to do this. Thus the Radio and Television Commission began, with Dr. Lowe serving as the first (and only) secretary of the commission.

As early as 1913, the Convention had a commission called the Social Service Commission whose purpose was to emphasize the Christian's responsibility in the complex social relations of modern life. In May, 1953, the name was changed to Christian Life Commisson, with headquarters in Nashville, Tennessee.

The origin of the Historical Commission may be dated to 1936 when the Convention named a special Committee on the Preservation of Baptist History. This was an able committee which took its work seriously and was soon enjoying a response to its efforts. In 1938, the Southern Baptist Historical Society was founded in Richmond, Virginia. The value of this project was soon recognized, so that in August, 1951, the Historical Commission was established as an agency of the Convention. Headquarters of this commission, along with the valuable library, are in Nashville, Tennessee.

The Baptist Brotherhood Commission grew out of a movement of laymen in the Convention at Richmond, Virginia, in 1907. This movement passed through several stages until it later became an official commission at the Convention of 1950.

For many years various individuals and groups had been emphasizing the doctrine of Christian stewardship. These various efforts were finally officially organized to become the Stewardship Commission of the Convention in 1960.

the whole world.

The above named boards and commissions are the agencies through which the work of the Southern Baptist Convention is done. It is a far cry from 1845, the day of beginnings, until 1975 when the official record showed a total of 12,735,663 members in 34,902 local congregations affiliated with the Southern Baptist Convention.

It might be said in conclusion that from the beginning Southern Baptists have considered Christian higher education as a vital agent of the Christian witness. As a matter of fact, several Southern Baptist colleges antedate the actual founding of the Southern Baptist Convention. Furman University was founded in 1825, Mississippi College in 1826, Georgetown College in 1829, University of Richmond in 1832, Mercer in 1833, Wake Forest in 1834, Judson College in 1838, Samford in 1841, and both Baylor and Mary Hardin-Baylor in the year the Convention was organized, 1845.

In *Baptist Faith and Message,* adopted by the Southern Baptist Convention in 1963, is the following statement:

> The cause of education in the Kingdom of Christ is coordinate with the causes of missions and general benevolence and should receive along with these the liberal support of the churches. An adequate system of Christian schools is necessary to a complete spiritual program for Christ's people.

SOUTHERN BAPTIST
EDUCATIONAL INSTITUTIONS

The Education Commission does not exercise any authority or control over institutions directly or indirectly. This position is in keeping with Baptist polity. Below is a list of the Baptist educational institutions showing the date founded and location.

SEMINARIES—

Golden Gate Baptist Theological Seminary, 1944; Strawberry Point; Mill Valley, California 94941

Midwestern Baptist Theological Seminary, 1957; 5001 North Oak Street Trafficway; Kansas City, Missouri 64118

New Orleans Baptist Theological Seminary, 1917; 3939 Gentilly Boulevard; New Orleans, Louisiana 70126

Southeastern Baptist Theological Seminary, 1951; Wake Forest, North Carolina 27587

Southern Baptist Theological Seminary, 1859; 2825 Lexington Road; Louisville, Kentucky 40206

Southwestern Baptist Theological Seminary, 1908; 2001 West Seminary Drive; Fort Worth, Texas 76122

SENIOR COLLEGES AND UNIVERSITIES—

Atlanta Baptist College, 1964; 3000 Flowers Road, N.E.; Atlanta, Georgia 30341 (Atlanta Campus of Mercer University)

Averett College, 1859; Danville, Virginia 24541

Baptist College at Charleston, 1964; P. O. Box 11087; Charleston, South Carolina 29411

Baylor University, 1845; Waco, Texas 76703

Belmont College, 1951; 1900 Belmont Boulevard; Nashville, Tennessee 37203

Bluefield College, 1922; Bluefield, Virginia 24605

Blue Mountain College, 1873; Blue Mountain, Mississippi 38610

California Baptist College, 1950; 8432 Magnolia Avenue; Riverside, California 92504

Campbell College, 1887; Buie's Creek, North Carolina 27506

Campbellsville College, 1907; Campbellsville, Kentucky 42718

Carson-Newman College, 1851; Jefferson City, Tennessee 37760

Cumberland College, 1888; Williamsburg, Kentucky 40769

Dallas Baptist College, 1965; Kiest Boulevard and Florine Drive (P. O. Box 2126); Dallas, Texas 75211

East Texas Baptist College, 1912; Marshall, Texas 75670
Furman University, 1825; Greenville, South Carolina 29613
Gardner-Webb College, 1905; Boiling Springs, North Carolina 28017
Georgetown College, 1829; Georgetown, Kentucky 40324
Grand Canyon College, 1949; 3300 West Camelback Road (P. O. Box 11097); Phoenix, Arizona 85017
Hardin-Simmons University, 1891; Abilene, Texas 79601

Meredith College, 1891; P. O. Box 409; Raleigh, North Carolina 27611
Mississippi College, 1826; Clinton, Mississippi 39056
Missouri Baptist College—Hannibal-LaGrange Campus, 1858; Hannibal, Missouri 63401—St. Louis Campus, 1963; 12542 Conway Road; St. Louis, Missouri 63141
Mobile College, 1961; College Parkway (P. O. Box 13220); Mobile, Alabama 36613
Oklahoma Baptist University, 1910; Shawnee, Oklahoma 74801
Ouachita Baptist University, 1885; Arkadelphia, Arkansas 71923
Palm Beach Atlantic College, 1966; 1101 South Olive Avenue; West Palm Beach, Florida 33401
Richmond, University of, 1832; Richmond, Virginia 23173
Samford University, 1841; Birmingham, Alabama 35209
Shorter College, 1873; Rome, Georgia 30161
Southwest Baptist College, 1878; Bolivar, Missouri 65613
Stetson University, 1883; DeLand, Florida 32720
Tift College, 1849; Forsyth, Georgia 31029
Union University, 1874; Jackson, Tennessee 38301
Virginia Intermont College, 1884; Bristol, Virginia 24201
Wake Forest University, 1834; Winston-Salem, North Carolina 27109
Wayland Baptist College, 1908; Plainview, Texas 79072
William Carey College, 1906; Hattiesburg, Mississippi 39401
William Jewell College, 1849; Liberty, Missouri 64068

7

JUNIOR COLLEGES—

Anderson College, 1911; Anderson, South Carolina 29621
Brewton-Parker College, 1904; Mt. Vernon, Georgia 30445
Chowan College, 1848; Murfreesboro, North Carolina 27855
Clarke College, 1908; Newton, Mississippi 39345
North Greenville College, 1892; Tigerville, South Carolina 29688
Southern Baptist College, 1941; Walnut Ridge, Arkansas 72476
Truett-McConnell College, 1946; Cleveland, Georgia 30528
Wingate College, 1895; Wingate, North Carolina 28174

ACADEMIES—

Acadia Baptist Academy, 1917; Eunice, Louisiana 70535
Fork Union Military Academy, 1898; Fork Union, Virginia 23055
Hargrave Military Academy, 1909; Chatham, Virginia 24531
Harrison-Chilhowee Baptist Academy, 1880; Seymour, Tennessee
    37865
Oak Hill Academy, 1878; Mouth of Wilson, Virginia 24363
Oneida Baptist Institute, 1899; Oneida, Kentucky 40972
San Marcos Baptist Academy, 1907; San Marcos, Texas 78666
Valley Baptist Academy, 1946; P. O. Box 1430; Harlingen, Texas
    78550

BIBLE SCHOOLS—

American Baptist College, 1924; 1800 White's Creek Pike; Nash-
    ville, Tennessee 37207*
Baptist Bible Institute, 1943; College Drive and 12th Avenue;
    Graceville, Florida 32440
Clear Creek Baptist School, 1926; Pineville, Kentucky 40977
Fruitland Baptist Institute, 1946; Hendersonville, North Carolina
    28739
Mexican Baptist Bible Institute, 1947; 8019 South Pan Am Ex-
    pressway; San Antonio, Texas 78224

---

* Supported jointly with National Baptist Convention, U.S.A., Incorporated.

CHAPTER II

Baptists' involvement in the field of higher education is usually surprised to discover how great an enterprise it now is. Baptists in this country were among the first church groups to establish colleges. As we have just pointed out in the previous chapter, some of these were in existence before the Convention itself was organized in 1845. Most of them were born in "hard times" and have struggled against inadequate financial resources during most of their history. Indeed, some have been unable to survive without adequate support. Those who have survived have done so through great sacrifice on the part of presidents, faculties, trustees, and interested friends. Nowhere among Baptists can one find better examples of heroic self-sacrifice than these devoted believers in higher education.

Today Southern Baptists own and control a total of 71 schools. Generally speaking, these are of two kinds: 1) those owned and operated by the Southern Baptist Convention (in this group are six theological seminaries); (2) those schools which are owned and operated by individual states in the Convention (these are usually classified as senior or four-year colleges, junior colleges, academies, and Bible schools).

These 71 schools are located by states as follows: Alabama 3, Arkansas 2, Arizona 1, California 2, Florida 3, Georgia 5, Kentucky 6, Louisiana 2, Mississippi 4, Missouri 5, North Carolina 9, Oklahoma 1, South Carolina 4, Tennessee 5, Texas 11, and Virginia 8.

9

Seminaries

In our consideration of these Baptist schools we shall deal first with those owned and operated by the southwide Convention; that is, the six Southern Baptist theological seminaries. Fortunately, even prior to 1845, there were among the Baptists in several southeastern states a number of well educated men, mostly ministers, who were instrumental in starting a program for the education of ministers. Among these were Richard Furman, William Bullein Johnson, John A. Broadus, James Petigru Boyce, Basil Manly, William Williams, and others. These were practical-minded men who were convinced that a trained ministry was a necessity. The first Southern Baptist college was established in South Carolina and named in honor of their great leader, Richard Furman. The most important department in this school was its theological department.

Out of this department the first Southern Baptist seminary came into being. The first session opened in Greenville, South Carolina, in 1859 with twenty-six students under the presidency of James Petigru Boyce. The school remained in Greenville for 18 years, but financial conditions in the South after the Civil War were so desperate that it became necessary to move. After serious consideration it was decided to move the young school to Louisville, Kentucky. The move was made in 1877, and Southern Baptist Seminary has continued to live in this Kentucky city.

For some forty years the Louisville institution was the only Southern Baptist seminary. Even before the Civil War, people in the South began moving westward. Texas attracted a great number of these, many of whom were Baptists. Among the early settlers were some educated men who soon began efforts to build Baptist schools. These efforts resulted in the founding of Baylor University in 1845. Since the chief concern of many of these leaders was an educated ministry, it was natural to establish a strong theological department at Baylor. This program prospered and for a time furnished trained leaders for the state. As the population of the state steadily increased, there arose a demand for a Baptist seminary in the state. This proposal involved lengthy discussions extending over several years. Finally an agreement was reached which resulted in the formal opening of Southwestern Baptist Theological Seminary in Fort Worth on October 3, 1908. The leading figure in this new school was B. H. Carroll. The school remained largely a Texas institution until 1925, when it became the second seminary of the Southern Baptist Convention.

The city of New Orleans, settled largely by French, Spanish, and later, Irish people, had long been almost overwhelmingly Roman Catholic. To the Baptists living in the city this Catholic predominance had constituted a real challenge. These few Baptist churches were weak and without substantial resources, but they never ~~~

support, were soon able to witness the establishing of the Baptist Bible Institute with Dr. B. H. Dement as first president in October, 1917. Despite hardships and various difficulties the institution continued to grow and was later taken over by the Southern Baptist Convention as its third seminary.

The next seminary to be approved and adopted by the Convention was located in Northern California and came to be known as the Golden Gate Baptist Theological Seminary. As early as 1850 some Southern Baptists were already moving to California. Among these were men who dreamed of establishing a Baptist school in the state. Some early efforts appeared hopeful but never did materialize. The migration to California continued, especially in the 1930s and during World War II. As the number of Baptists increased, the demand for a seminary became more urgent. Isom B. Hodges took the lead, assisted by Dallas G. Faulkner. With the help of several churches the Golden Gate Southern Baptist Theological Seminary was incorporated under the laws of the state of California on July 12, 1944. With Hodges serving as president, the first session opened in Oakland on September 20, 1944. Three years later the school moved to Berkeley, where it remained until the trustees purchased the magnificent campus where it now stands in beautiful Mill Valley. In January, 1951, this new seminary began getting its support from the Southern Baptist Convention.

As Baptists continued to grow in numbers after World War II, the seminary in Louisville was becoming crowded. About this time there developed the feeling that the thickly populated region in the southeastern part of the country needed a seminary. Survey committees were appointed and finally brought to the Convention a hearty recommendation that a fifth seminary should be established. Inasmuch as Wake Forest College was soon to move to Winston-Salem, North Carolina, arrangements were made to purchase this campus as the site for the new school. The Convention authorized the new seminary at its meeting in Chicago in May, 1950, and appointed the first board of trustees. Class work was begun on the Wake Forest campus in September, 1951. Arrangements were made for both schools to occupy the campus until the college could complete its move to Winston-Salem. The move was completed in 1956, and since that time Southeastern Baptist Seminary has occupied this historic campus. Under the able leadership of its first president, Dr. S. L. Stealey, the school flourished.

As the number of ministerial students among Southern Baptists continued to grow, Baptists in the Midwest expressed a strong desire for a seminary in this area. The Convention authorized the appointment of proper committees to make thorough survey of the needs and the prospects of such a venture. The outcome was the hearty recommendation that a sixth seminary be located in Kansas City, Missouri. This recommendation was voted by the Convention in Chicago on May 29, 1957, and the first board of trustees was elected. In June, 1957, the trustees held their first meeting in Kansas City, Missouri, to begin work on this new enterprise. The trustees met again on October 8, 1957, and elected as the first president of Midwestern Baptist Theological Seminary Dr. Millard J. Berquist, then pastor of the First Baptist Church of Tampa, Florida. The first classes in this sixth Southern Baptist Theological Seminary were held early in September, 1958.

Each of these seminaries is directed by a board of trustees which is elected by the Southern Baptist Convention. These trustees elect a president, the faculty, and other officials. Trustees also handle, at regular meetings, all matters of policy. The president submits a carefully detailed report to each annual meeting of the Convention.

Some twenty-five years ago the seminaries initiated a program which is providing courses of study for more than 8,000 students annually. Ministers and laymen who have not gone to a seminary now have courses brought to them through the Seminary Extension Department. This is a comprehensive program sponsored by the six seminaries and directed by Dr. Raymond M. Rigdon with head-quarters in Nashville, Tennessee.

Colleges and Schools

We are to consider now the general nature, purpose, and opera-tion of the various schools which are controlled and supported by the Baptist conventions in various states. Here we have a uniqu

cerned with the religious life of its students. Of course, tax-supported schools and universities can assume no responsibility in this area. To maintain high academic standards for accreditation and at the same time be genuinely Christian in ideals and practice is far from easy. However, what has been done and is being done by Baptist schools demonstrates that it is abundantly worthwhile.

Since Baptists (and other Christian bodies) were free to establish their own academies and colleges, they began building schools even before the Southern Baptist Convention was established in 1845. Of the 45 senior colleges now operating in the Southern Baptist Convention, fifteen of these were founded between 1825 (when Furman was established) and the Civil War. For the most part the junior colleges, academies, and Bible schools came after 1900.

Two ideas were usually in the forefront in establishing Baptist schools. First was the desire to provide facilities for educating minis-ters. This motive can be detected in the history of practically all of these institutions. Some schools were begun as missionary enter-prises. For example, in mountain regions or other isolated areas, the building of an academy where young ministers could study made it feasible for these young men to preach in communities nearby and thus win converts and add members to the churches. It is only fair to state that a considerable number of these small schools were unable to live. There were various reasons for failure. In the first place, in some situations which did not offer the pros-pect of enduring, perhaps it was unwise to undertake such a project. As public high schools gradually became available to practically all regions, the need for most of these academies passed. Certainly a good number died for lack of financial support. However, there remain seven Baptist academies whose outlook is much brighter. It is to be noted that in all parts of the nation there is a resurgent growth of private secondary schools.

In addition, the state conventions give encouragement and support to four Bible schools. These provide organized Bible study for ministers who for various reasons have not been able to get formal training.

The work of these colleges, academies and Bible schools is done through trustees elected by the Baptist state conventions, and by administrators and faculty members elected by the trustees. This method assures the Baptist people that their work is properly administered.

The writer wishes that it were possible to give many interesting facts about these colleges and schools but since this is impossible, we are presenting some statistics which will give the reader some idea of what is involved in the program of higher education among Southern Baptists. The figures are taken from the report of Dr. Ben C. Fisher, executive director-treasurer of the Education Commission, at the meeting of the Southern Baptist Convention in Kansas City, June, 1977.

A. Six Southern Baptist Theological Seminaries
    Total number of faculty and administrative
    officers 381

    Total number of students (including Seminary
    Extension) 18,649

    Total number of volumes in libraries 855,083

    Total value of property and endowment ...... $ 86,880,991

B. Southern Baptist Senior Colleges
    Total number of faculty and administrative
    officers 4,944

    Total number of students enrolled 119,363

    Total number of volumes in libraries 5,832,267

    Total value of property and endowment ....$ 892,528,769

C. Southern Baptist Junior Colleges
Total number of faculty and administrative
officers 388
Total number of students enrolled 9,990
Total number of volumes in libraries 272,190
Total value of property and endowment ......$ 48,320,935

officers 65
Total number of students 1,726
Total number of volumes in libraries 76,850
Total value of property and endowment ....$ 6,831,238

By adding these four figures from each of the five types of Southern Baptist schools we find a total:
Faculty and administrative officers 5,993
Number of students enrolled 152,579
Number of volumes in libraries 7,100,902
Value of property and endowment $1,058,189,004

Southern Baptists may be justifiably proud of their assets in the field of higher education.

At a later point in this volume we shall attempt to give an appraisal of these Baptist schools. At this point it seems appropriate to speak briefly of the quality of the men and women who give leadership to this worthy enterprise. This writer may be permitted a personal word in this connection. He became a member of the Education Commission of the Convention in 1936. For 40 years he has attended from one to four meetings of these Baptist educators each year. He has come to know perhaps as many as 200 of these men and women during these years. One could never know a company of choicer servants of Jesus Christ. Baptists can trust them fully—and should support them heartily.

CHAPTER III

In these discussions we have spoken frequently of a "commission" of the Southern Baptist Convention. The matter is important enough to merit some examination. In a word, a commission is a group of men and women elected by the Convention to deal officially with a specific field of work in the program of the Convention. The following quotation concerning the purpose and the work of the Education Commission is taken from the Commission's program statement.

> The purpose of the Education Commission is to provide materials, counsel, and information to the agencies of the Southern Baptist Convention for their periodicals, publications, and other services to the churches; to provide specific services to Baptist seminaries, colleges, and schools; to provide specific information to Baptist pastors and churches about the services offered by our Baptist laymen who are in higher education in schools other than Baptist; to promote cooperation between the educational institutions and the agencies of the Southern Baptist Convention; to maintain liaison with regional accrediting associations, the United States Office of Education, state boards of higher education, boards of higher education in other religious bodies, and professional educational organizations and learned societies.

Essentially this is the operation of the principle of democracy in religion. Baptists have no ecclesiastical authorities who alone make decisions and then hand down orders to lesser individuals to put into operation. Rather, an effort is made to involve "the brethren" in free discussion of a matter, with the conviction that the combined wisdom and judgment of a group of selected people is far better than the decisions of any one individual. For example, the judgments of the seventeen members of the Education Commission, arrived at after full discussion, are far safer than the opinions of any one man. Furthermore, the fact that men have been involved in decision-making helps to assure their support (and that of their friends).

In the Convention the commission plan was first used in 1915 when the Education Commission was created, though the principle is the same as that employed by certain "boards" from the beginning. As time passed and needs arose, other commissions have been established by the Convention until there are now seven.

Members to fill vacancies in these commissions are nominated by the committee on boards of the Southern Baptist Convention. After their nomination the Convention casts its vote. Following the Convention session, the clerk sends notice of election to each member. The Convention plan of rotation is followed so that no member may serve longer than two terms in succession. After the expiration of at least one year, a member may be elected again.

In the Education Commission there are seventeen members: one from each state in which a Baptist school is located, plus one "at-large member."

There are no stated qualifications for membership. Of course it is assumed that a prospective member should be an intelligent, respected leader. It is obviously desirable, also, that the member be vitally interested in the field in which he is to work.

To be an effective member of this commission requires dedication and intelligent effort. While it is an honor to serve on a commission, the real purpose is to make a contribution to its work. The ideal member attends all meetings faithfully and always serves when asked to do so. He is expected to serve on committees and to do extra work when it is necessary. He supports the executive director-treasurer in carrying out Education Commission policy. A commission member's position calls for study and involvement over the entire year, not simply at formal meetings. He has the obligation of keeping the people of his state informed on the work of the commission.

Each commission meets in business session at least once each year. Special meetings may be held when there is occasion. The actions and recommendations of the group are usually included in the report which the executive director-treasurer makes to the

sion. He is selected and employed by the commission members after careful investigation and consultation. The terms of his contract are mutually agreed upon, and he is accountable to the commission alone.

Perhaps in none of the several commissions of the Convention are the qualifications so professional as in this one. In short, this executive director-treasurer must be a specialist in the field of higher education. He should be academically qualified (preferably from a Baptist or denominational college) and should have wide experience in the field of higher education. Equally essential is his knowledge of what is going on in this field in the whole country today. Keeping current is not easy, since significant changes are constantly taking place. The members of the commission cannot be specialists; the director must be the interpreter and the leader in this area. In educational matters he represents not only the commission but in a real sense Southern Baptists as well. As in foreign missions affairs, people look to the executive secretary of the Foreign Mission Board for leadership, just so the executive director-treasurer of the Education Commission is expected to speak with authority.

It is highly desirable that this leader in higher education be a loyal denominational man. He must work with all the boards and commissions of the Convention. His field of activity is no less denominational than that of the executives of other commissions and boards. Unfortunately, there are some who have the notion that even colleges and seminaries which are designated as Baptist are really not an essential part of the denominational world program. The schools resent such thinking and insist on being a member of the "team." In recent years the Education Commission through leadership of Dr. Ben C. Fisher, the executive director-treasurer, has made remarkable progress in establishing closer working relations with the various agencies of the Southern Baptist Convention, especially with the Foreign Mission Board, the Home Mission Board, the Sunday School Board, and Woman's Missionary Union, all of which need the services of colleges and seminaries in training future leaders in their work. It is gratifying to see the eager and hearty response of these agencies in cooperating with the Education Commission.

A reading of the annual report of the Education Commission to the Southern Baptist Convention will give the reader some idea of the varied duties the executive director-treasurer is expected to discharge. A later chapter in this volume will deal more at length with these duties; however, one can easily see that the responsibilities demand a wide variety of skills. The director is expected to be a congenial co-worker with leaders in other fields, to be a pleasing and effective speaker on many occasions, and to write numerous reports, which must be accurate and appropriate. The conducting of varied seminars and conferences demands time and expertise. Leading special meetings designed to keep trustees of the schools informed has recently become a responsibility of the director. At all times, one or more of these three-score-and-ten schools will be having special problems and difficulties and will be looking to the director for special counsel. Sometimes it is his function "to pour oil on troubled waters." As treasurer of the commission he is responsible for its budget and the wise expenditure of this money, and the handling of certain scholarship funds entrusted to the commission. The direction of personnel for the routine operation of the office naturally is the responsibility of the director of the commission.

The Southern Baptist Convention has greatly increased its support of the work of the Education Commission. In 1970 the Cooperative Program support for the commisson was $125,000. By the year 1977-78, this contribution is $250,000, a one hundred percent rise.

Three other matters need to be noted. For a number of years the Education Commsision has administered the Opdyke Fund, the income from which is assigned to Baptist colleges to be used as scholarships for needy students from the Southern Appalachian mountains. Since 1961 this fund has produced more than $350,-000 in income and has assisted 483 students. The Dorothea Van Deusen Opdyke Fund was established in a bequest left to the Southern Baptist Convention by Mrs. Ida Reed Opdyke of James-

grading teaching skills. Almost 200 teachers have been assisted by these funds.

This brief treatment of the functions of the Education Commission should give one some understanding of the significance of the work of the Education Commission today.

CHAPTER IV

We are now to look at the history of this commission which has to do with higher education among Southern Baptists. First, we will deal with the beginning of the commission and its work up to the time (1951) when the first salaried secretary or director was employed. The other chapters will bring the story up to the present.

We have already noted that the Southern Baptist Convention as a body was not involved in the founding of any colleges, academies or Bible schools. Officially the Convention was concerned only with theological seminaries. This policy simply followed the pattern established in early years when the individual states built and sponsored their own academies, colleges and Bible schools.

The immediate objective in establishing these Baptist schools was to provide educational facilities for ministers. At first the majority of students in these schools were young ministers. However, as the benefits of higher education became apparent, students other than ministers came in ever-increasing numbers.

Naturally, some of these schools were too hastily conceived and could not survive; just how many finally died, we have no way of knowing. Others not only survived but prospered. By the beginning of the twentieth century, higher education among Southern Baptists had become a big enterprise. These schools had a vast potential for the denomination. Leaders of the Convention began to feel that the Convention needed the schools and could give them assistance and encouragement.

Clearly the time had come for the Convention to take some action. The first expressed move in this direction came at the meeting of the Convention in Chattanooga in May, 1906, when the following motion was made by P. T. Hale of Tennessee:

> That a Committee of five be appointed upon the subject of General Denominational Education within our bounds. This Committee shall be instructed, first, to gather statistics and other information which a broad study of the field shall yield; second, to confer with the Committee on Order of Business at the next session of this body and arrange a time at which this report shall be submitted to the Convention next year.[1]

This committee reported at the session of 1908, making several suggestions, such as closer relations between the various schools, caution in founding new colleges, and better financing of these institutions. Apparently not much came out of this study.

However, a committee which had been appointed at the Convention in St. Louis in 1913 stated in the Convention at Houston in 1915 that "It is apparent to us as we doubt not it is to the Convention that we must take hold of our educational task in a new and larger way if we are to keep pace with times in which we live and meet the needs of our situation."[2] This committee was continued, and at the Convention at Asheville in May, 1916, gave a long, detailed report showing the need for a commission to do the work which seemed imperative. In their report we find the statement, "We, therefore, recommend that the Convention appoint an Education Commission composed of one member from each state."[3] Since the committee appointed in 1915 to make this study and recommendation is called in the minutes the "Education Commission," it is not clear whether the commission came into existence in 1915 at Houston or in 1916 at Asheville. Dr. Charles D. Johnson, in his book *Higher Education of Southern Baptists,* states that the commission began at Houston in 1915. It was the intention of this committee of 1915 that the Convention should establish an education *board* on a par with other boards of the Convention. Instead, the new title was *commission*. However, as we shall see, this body was later replaced by an Education Board.

The new Education Commission took its task seriously and began its work, as Dr. Johnson's history states:

> For four years this Commission, under the author-
>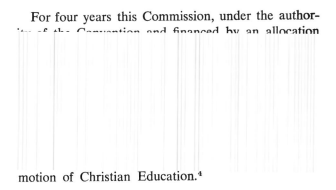
> motion of Christian Education.[4]

The work of the commission expanded so rapidly that it was felt that this task could be satisfactorily accomplished only by an education board. The commission itself recommended this action to the Convention, and the Convention adopted a resolution creating the Education Board. The new board, created in 1919, was begun on an impressive scale.

This new Education Board established headquarters in Birmingham, Alabama. Several staff members were employed, and Dr. J. E. Dillard, pastor of the Southside Baptist Church in Birmingham, agreed to serve as secretary until a permanent secretary could be found.

At the meeting of the Convention in 1920, Dr. Dillard presented an impressive report, in which sixteen specific recommendations were made. Without attempting to quote all of these in detail, we may select several to show how thoroughly Dr. Dillard had surveyed the field:

1. Maintain a clearinghouse of educational matters for the use of administrative officers of the colleges.

2. Cooperate with all boards of the Convention.

3. Work constantly toward the enlightenment of the Baptist constituency.

4. Conserve Baptist interests in colleges and universities.

5. Study constantly the curricula and academic standards of Baptist schools.

6. Prepare materials for enlisting students who should enter special Christian vocations.

7. Assist Baptist schools in making requests for financial aid.

8. Conduct a campaign for large gifts.

9. Establish a teachers' bureau.

10. Provide a system for scholarships.

In this same report it was recommended that the board be organized in three departments: (1) Publicity and Propaganda, (2) College Department, and (3) Student Department. By 1924 the work of the board was grouped under seven departments: (1) Surveys, (2) Publicity, (3) Institutions, (4) Student Life, (5) Teachers' Bureau, (6) Legal and Legislative, and (7) Standardization and Promotion.

Dr. William Carey James assumed the office of corresponding secretary, July 1, 1920. After four years, Dr. James resigned to become president of Bethel College. Dr. J. W. Cammack served from October 1, 1924, to May 19, 1927. Dr. Rufus W. Weaver served from October 7, 1927, until the board was discontinued by Convention vote in 1928. Dr. Albert R. Bond served as editorial secretary from August 1, 1920, to January, 1927.

A big financial venture of the board to raise $15,000,000 for the schools was of extraordinary significance. We quote from Dr. Johnson's history:

> A most significant change took place in the movement first championed by the original Education Commission and then by its logical successor, the Education Board, to raise $15,000,000 for Christian education by merging plans for Christian education with the Seventy-Five Million Campaign. The Southern Baptist Convention, whose special emphasis had been in all previous years upon evangelism and missions, was now ready to participate in a co-operative movement to endow Baptist colleges and to assist in

26

financing sorely needed building programs. Also, since many Baptist colleges were seriously handicapped by debt, it was contemplated that merging activities of educational forces—including educational agencies of Baptist state conventions—with the Seventy-Five Million Campaign would accomplish in five years more for all Southern Baptist work than could

and endowment income estimates upon receiving the full amount of the anticipated funds found themselves still in debt and not sufficiently endowed. Building programs were then either discontinued or, if completed, additional indebtedness was incurred.[5]

As indicated in the above statement by Dr. Johnson, financial conditions were becoming serious and people were alarmed by the debts of some agencies of the Southern Baptist Convention. The report of the Education Board to the Convention meeting at Chattanooga in May, 1928, was a long one of 35 pages (369-404). In this the financial standing of the Education Board was given in detail. After an extended discussion (some 15 or more men participating), a resolution offered by Charles E. Maddry was adopted. The substance of the resolution was to discontinue the Education Board, and in its place set up an Education Commission on a much less expensive scale. The introduction to the resolution states: "While reaffirming our abiding interest in Christian Education and our loyalty to our Baptist schools, yet, under existing financial conditions in our general missionary and benevolent work, we feel that the following changes in our methods of promoting education are desirable."[6]

The resolution called for the Executive Committee of the Convention to be recognized as the "successor in law" to the Board of Education. This meant that the properties and obligations of the board should be transferred to the Executive Committee of the Convention. The board ceased its actual operations on October 1, 1928, but in order to complete the transfer of properties and obligations, it was necessary to continue the board as a legal entity until 1932. The Executive Committee carried an account on its books in the name of the board until June 15, 1938.

It should be noted that early in its existence the board became the holder of a principal interest in the Ridgecrest Baptist Assembly. Since it held a majority of the stock, it controlled the operations of the assembly until June, 1938.

In his article on the Education Board in the *Encyclopedia of Southern Baptists,* R. Orin Cornett summarized the financial record of the board as follows:

> During its nine years as a functioning organization, the board received from all denominational sources $2,214,756.67, and disbursed to denominational causes and institutions $2,588,417.41. Its receipts for its own work totaled $228,183.49. Indebtedness at the time it ceased operation was $387,442.40, including $106,787.79 (in excess of receipts for this purpose) advanced to colleges and seminaries, plus $27,142.62 accumulated interest on same and $216,743.95 spent on improvements to the Ridgecrest Assembly property, plus $42,768.14 accumulated interest and bond issue expense. Property value totaled $799,929.34, including: Ridgecrest Assembly, $605,416.84, Nuyaka Indian School, $80,000.00, Umatilla (Florida Assembly) $114,512.50.[7]

Thus it was that the Education Board of the Southern Baptist Convention was officially discontinued after some eight years of work. While the chief factor in its dissolution was financial, it is true that some other factors were involved. Since it was a new venture in the life of the denomination, some of its efforts were experimental and naturally caused some misunderstanding. It is true also that the majority of Baptist people were not yet convinced of the need of higher education and thus were not ready to support the programs attempted by the board. There were some who felt that the board began its work on too ambitious a scale. Certainly it did have difficulty in defining and establishing its proper area of service within the pattern of activities of Convention agencies.

All four corresponding secretaries (Drs. Dillard, James, Cammack, and Weaver) were competent, dedicated men. As pioneers in a new field, they and the members of the board were zealous and enthusiastic in their labors. We can understand how some mistakes would be made in such a venture. In view of what was accomplished in these eight years.

Dr. Charles D. Johnson:

> The Education Board, the first agency created by the Southern Baptist Convention whose sole purpose was to promote education, was highly successful in bringing to the attention of all Baptist denominational agencies—Southwide and state—the existing conditions in all Southern Baptist educational institutions. Meanwhile, too, the values in Christian schools were set forth in annual reports to the Southern Baptist Convention and to Baptist state conventions in such meaningful descriptions and statistical tabulations that a Christian educational conscience was being developed through all the territory of the Southern Baptist Convention. This conscience became the basis upon which leaders in future campaigns could rely for active and effective participation.[8]

At the meeting of the Southern Baptist Convention in Chattanooga in May, 1928, the resolution which called for the discontinuing of the Education Board called also for the creating of an Education Commission to take its place. This commission was to be "composed of one member from each state." In this way, the second Education Commission of the Southern Baptist Convention came into existence. The members of the new commission were named and had their first meeting during the ensuing year.

As we trace the work of this "second" commission in its early years we are to follow the record as given by Dr. Charles D. Johnson, who served as chairman of the commission for twenty-one years (1932-1953). In his monumental volume *Higher Education of Southern Baptists,* written at the request of the Education Commission, he gives the record of events and accomplishments of this commission during these years up to 1954. This is the only authentic connected record in existence. We are making liberal use of his material and, of course, give Dr. Johnson full credit for this.

It is exceedingly fortunate that Dr. Johnson was on hand and was willing to assume leadership of the commission at this time.

Charles D. Johnson was then on the faculty of Baylor University. A native of Mississippi, he graduated from Mississippi College with the A.B. and A.M. degrees. He did graduate work at Johns Hopkins University, Missouri University, and Iowa University, where he was awarded the Ph.D. degree in 1921.

His professional career included six years as professor and four as president of Ouachita College, three years as professor at Arkansas A. & M. College, two as professor and dean at Blue Mountain College, and twenty-three at Baylor Unversity. In 1950 Mississippi College conferred on him the honorary degree of LL.D., and in 1952 Mercer University conferred on him the honorary degree of LL.D.

It would be difficult to overstate the magnitude of the contribution made by Dr. Johnson to Baptist schools during more than twenty years of sacrificial labor. When the Education Board was abolished, the commission was without official headquarters, with no secretarial help, and with only a very modest expense account. Dr. Johnson served all these years without a salary. Literally he did whatever had to be done. Along with him as faithful colleague and personal friend was Dr. Spright Dowell, president of Mercer University, who served as secretary-treasurer. The other members of the commission were cooperative and did what they could, but it is not too much to say that these were the men who bore the responsibility, who furnished inspiration, and who refused to give up. Without them the whole venture might have failed. As we continue the story, let us remember the hard situation in which these heroic leaders worked.

As before stated, the Southern Baptist Convention abolished the Education Board and then created the "second" Education Commission in 1928. Dr. Johnson's history of Southern Baptist higher education describes the transition.

The report of E. B. Hatcher for the committee on the report of the Education Board follows:

The report of the Education Board has set forth the work of the past year and the large and inviting field of op

circulated a large and valuable array of facts bearing upon our Southern Baptist educational situation and his work should be held in grateful appreciation by our Convention.

2. The Convention in its decision to discontinue the Education Board, while causing disappointment to many, yet sounded a note for Christian education which should enlist all our hearts, and unite us for a new co-operation. The Convention has reaffirmed its profound interest in Christian education. It has appointed an agency for its promotion. Let us, therefore, join hearts and hands in a new effort to kindle in all our people a more hearty and liberal interest in the great cause. If we will do this, then our Baptist Schools, which it is said, furnish 90 per cent of our pastors, missionaries and leaders, will find an ever higher place in the heart of Southern Baptists and a bright day will dawn on our educational sky.

Membership of the new Education Commission consisted of one representative from each of the eighteen states in the territory of the Southern Baptist Convention and the District of Columbia, a plan identical with that used for the now discontinued Education Board. That board had functioned with a corresponding secretary, an editorial secretary, and steno-

31

graphic assistants. Offices in Birmingham served as headquarters. The new Commission was furnished an [annual] expense fund of $2,500 to be used in carrying out the purposes set forth in the resolution which had created the commission. This fund was deemed sufficient to defray the expenses of an annual Christian Education Conference at Ridgecrest, a business session at the close of the Conference, the purchasing of stationery and postage necessary to conduct correspondence; and to print a minimum of bulletins to mail to Baptist seminaries, colleges and universities, junior colleges and academies; to Baptist state headquarters, to Baptist newspapers; and to pay for the services of a part-time office secretary. There was no salaried officer and no office was provided for headquarters. The chairman, elected by the Commission, performed administrative duties on a voluntary basis; the secretary-treasurer performed the duties of custodian of funds and wrote all checks, upon presentation of itemized accounts, with the written approval of the chairman. An audit at the end of each year was submitted to the Executive Board of the Southern Baptist Convention.

The assembling, interpreting, publishing, and distributing of educational information and the arrangement for, and conduct of, educational conferences provided a task of considerable proportions during those years in which there was no executive secretary. At least one man, academically and professionally qualified, was imperative for the work. This responsibility fell logically upon the chairman. Dr. Harry Clark was the first chairman and served one year. Dr. W. R. Cullom was the second chairman and served one year. Dr. Charles D. Johnson was elected chairman the third year and served for twenty-one years.[9]

Shortly after becoming chairman of the commission, Dr. Johnson suggested that members be asked to accept appointments as members of subcommittees. The following committees were named: standards, survey and statistics, reports and programs, interrelationships, and publicity. This proved to be a fortunate arrangement which challenged the members and gave continuity to the program.

In the meantime the severe depression had come upon the country. The very meager expense fund of $2,500 per year was reduced to $1,000. At the meeting of the Convention in Washington, D.C., in 1935, even this allocation was omitted. Had it not been for the strong appeal made by Chairman Johnson, the commission would have been left with no operating expenses and might have folded up. But these dedicated men persisted in their work, and their program gradually won support and gained popular favor.

One of the most significant developments was the founding of

should make every effort to be fully accredited academically. In various ways this policy was emphasized and encouraged by the commission. The result is that Southern Baptist colleges and schools are now accredited by either the Southern Association of Colleges and Secondary Schools, the North Central Association of Colleges and Secondary Schools, or the Western Association of Colleges and Secondary Schools. This fact has proved to be of tremendous significance academically.

The commission has encouraged a closer working relationship between the colleges and the six seminaries. These seminaries are now a vital part of the program of the Education Commission among Southern Baptists.

As the work of the commission prospered and gained momentum, some presidents and deans of colleges felt the need for an organization in which these college officials could meet at least once a year for fellowship, stimulating addresses, and serious discussion of problems and issues. A called meeting of the commission was held in Memphis on November 29, 1948. At the time of the founding the official name was the Southern Association of Baptist Colleges and Schools. This was later changed to the Association of Southern Baptist Colleges and Schools in order not to be in conflict with the Southern Association of Colleges and Schools. This new organization was in no sense in opposition to the commission but in support of it. The association is now a vigorous organization which sponsors excellent annual programs and works in complete harmony with the commission. As a matter of fact, the Education Commission at present does the staff work for the association. A list of those who have served as presidents of the Association of Southern Baptist Colleges and Schools is found in the Appendix of this book.

Chairman Johnson frequently spoke of the desirability of having Southern Baptist scholars write textbooks for college use. His concern resulted in at least one successful venture. The commission authorized Dr. H. I. Hester of William Jewell College to write a text for the study of the Old Testament, and a year later a text for the New Testament. These were published in 1949 and 1950, have been purchased by over 400 schools of several denominations, and are still widely used in colleges and schools and in churches for advanced study.

It seems fitting to close this chapter on the work of the Education Commission under the leadership of Chairman Charles D. Johnson by quoting the excellent summary written by Dr. R. Orin Cornett, who became the first salaried secretary of the commission just two years before Dr. Johnson retired:

> Despite the handicap of a very limited budget covering only expenses of meetings and the cost of correspondence, the commission contributed, during the period of Johnson's chairmanship, guidance and encouragement at many vital points. Its consistent emphasis upon standardization and upon the need for qualified, consecrated faculty, and its never-ceasing campaign to stir the educational conscience of Southern Baptists were invaluable in a period in which the fortunes of Southern Baptist educational institutions were repeatedly at stake. Its role as an official voice for Christian higher education was particularly valuable during the stressful years of the depression, when school after school encountered financial problems without precedent. By focusing attention upon specific needs and problems as they became acute, the commission accomplished during this period results which were far out of proportion to the meager financial outlay involved.[10]

FOOTNOTES, CHAPTER IV

[1] *Annual of the Southern Baptist Convention,* 1906, p. 39 (Item 90).

[2] *Annual of the Southern Baptist Convention,* 1915, p. 76 (Item 121).

[3] *Annual of the Southern Baptist Convention,* 1916, p. 56 (Item 72).

[4] Charles D. Johnson, *Higher Education of Southern Baptists* (Waco, Texas: Baylor University Press, 1955), pp. 47-48.

[5] *Ibid.,* pp. 49-50.

[6] *Annual of the Southern Baptist Convention,* 1928, p. 53 (Item 45).

[7] *Encyclopedia of Southern Baptists, Volume I* (Nashville, Tennessee:

CHAPTER V

During the dreary years of the depression Southern Baptist colleges and schools managed to survive with but few casualties. In the exciting and uncertain years of World War II they likewise continued to serve. During these critical times the Education Commission had demonstrated its worth, and the quality and extent of its service was now becoming recognized not only by the schools themselves but by denominational leaders also.

In the meantime leaders of the commission were becoming aware of the needs and the opportunities faced by the colleges and schools in the postwar period. As financial conditions improved, the commission optimistically planned for enlarging its ministry. Any expansion of its service would call for a full-time salaried staff member. A request for a larger appropriation received a favorable hearing, and additional funds were made available.

The commission now proceeded to choose its first executive secretary-treasurer. After careful investigation the members elected Dr. R. Orin Cornett, who at the time was executive vice-president of Oklahoma Baptist University. He began his work on February 1, 1951, in the newly established office of the commission in Nashville, Tennessee. At last the commission was in a position to work comfortably and effectively at its big task. Fortunately, Chairman

Johnson served for two years after Dr. Cornett began his work. Upon Dr. Johnson's retirement as chairman, special recognition was given him for his long and distinguished service.

R. Orin Cornett is a native of Oklahoma. He was graduated from Oklahoma Baptist University with the B.S. degree in 1934. Later he received the M.S. degree from Oklahoma University, and in 1940 was awarded the Ph.D. degree in physics from the University of Texas. In 1950 he became executive vice-president of Oklahoma Baptist University.

Dr. Cornett was well equipped for his work as executive secretary of the Education Commission. Young, vigorous and enthusiastic, he began his work with zest. He was wholly committed to the Christian philosophy of higher education. He was loyal to his denomination and worked amicably with other Baptist leaders. He was alert and creative in his thinking. Many of the basic projects launched during his administration are still employed in the program of the commission.

One of the first and most important ventures launched by Dr. Cornett was the securing of the charter of incorporation of the commission. This was dated December 10, 1951, under the laws of Tennessee. Because this charter is basic in the work of the Education Commission we are including it in this chapter.

CHARTER OF INCORPORATION

I

The name of the Corporaton shall be EDUCATION COMMISSION OF THE SOUTHERN BAPTIST CONVENTION.

II

The principal office of the Corporation shall be in the City of Nashville, in the State of Tennessee.

III

The Corporation is organized for educational and benevolent purposes and not for profit, hence no capital stock shall be required or issued, and no dividends or profits shall be divided among the members of the Corporation. It is established:

To serve the educational interests of the Southern Baptist Convention through services to educational institutions and by the making of gifts, donations, and benefactions, by deed, by will, by gift or otherwise, for the advancement, promotion, extension and

world.

IV

The period of duration of this Corporation shall be perpetual, with the right to terminate its corporate existence in a manner prescribed by the laws of the State of Tennessee.

The members may, by and with the approval of the Southern Baptist Convention, at any time voluntarily dissolve the Corporation by a conveyance of its assets and property to any other corporation holding a charter from the State for purposes not of individual profit, first providing for corporate debts. A violation of any of the provisions of the charter shall subject the Corporaton to dissolution at the instance of the State of Tennessee.

V

The affairs of this Corporation shall be managed by a Board of Directors consisting of one person from each state in which is located an academic educational institution owned, controlled or given substantial monetary support by a state convention or state general association of Baptists recognized as affiliated with the Southern Baptist Convention, plus one member selected from the Southern Baptist Convention territory as member-at-large.

VI

The persons named in the Charter as Incorporators shall be members of the first Board of Directors of the Corporation, and they, together with others chosen by the Southern Baptist Convention in accord with the provisions of Article V, shall hold office until their successors, or the successors of any of them, are chosen by the Southern Baptist Convention.

VII

The general powers of the Corporation shall be:

1. To take, receive, own, hold, administer, distribute, and dispose of properties of all kinds whether real, personal, or mixed, acquired by gift, bequest, devise, purchase, or otherwise; and to do any other thing incident thereto.

2. To sue and be sued by corporate name; to administer such property, to convey the same by sale or otherwise; to invest and reinvest it or the proceeds thereof in such manner as the judgment of the Directors may determine, but subject always to the following restrictions:

(a) In every case where specific instructions shall have been given the Directors of the Commission by the donor, grantor, or testator, the trust gift shall be known as a "designated gift," and the instruction shall be forever binding upon this Corporation and its successors and shall be carried out.

(b) The Corporation shall not have the right to mortgage, hypothecate, or otherwise pledge the real, personal, or mixed properties known as a "designated gift," under the ownership and control of the Corporation, except that it may refinance or renew any indebtedness that may exist at the time that the ownership or management of said properties pass to the Corporation.

(c) In the absence of specific instructions from the donor, grantor, or testator, the trust gift shall be known as an "undesignated gift," and the Corporation may borrow money by mortgage, pledge,

or recommendation of the Southern Baptist Convention or the Executive Committee of the Southern Baptist Convention.

3. To make all bylaws, rules, and regulations necessary to the transaction of the business of the Corporation, not inconsistent with the Laws of the State of Tennessee, or of the United States of America.

4. To have and use a common seal which may be altered at pleasure. If no common seal, then the signature of the name of the Corporation by any duly authorized officer, acting with authority, shall be legal and binding.

5. No change may be made in this Charter except with the prior authority of the Southern Baptist Convention. This Charter may be amended according to the provision of the Laws of the State of Tennessee governing General Welfare Charter, without legislative consent.

6. To appoint such subordinate officers and agents in addition to the President or Chairman, Vice-President or Vice-Chairman, and Secretary or Treasurer as the business of the Corporation may require. Due notice of any election must be given by a letter

41

mailed to the last known address of said directors ten (10) days preceding the meeting, or a day stated on the minutes of the Board of Directors.

7. To designate the name of the officers and fix the compensation of the officers.

8. To select from the Board of Directors five (5) of their number as an Administrative Committee. The chairman of this committee shall be either the President or Vice-President of the Corporation. The Board of Directors may delegate to the Administrative Committee whatever general powers they elect to confer and full authority with reference to the investments, re-investments and administration of the principal and income of all funds and property devised, bequeathed, given or transferred to the Corporation with authority to execute property transfers, assignments, contracts, deeds, releases, acquittances, and any and all instruments that may be necessary in the administration of the property and assets of the Corporation.

9. There shall be no individual liability against the members, for corporate debts, but the entire corporate property shall be liable for the claims of creditors subject to restrictions under Article VII and subsections 2, (a) and (b) thereof.

For the record we are listing the names of the men who have served as chairman of the commission from the beginning up to the present.

1929-30	Harry Clark
1930-31	W. R. Cullom
1932-53	Charles D. Johnson
1954	Spright Dowell
1955	Charles L. Harman
1956	Warren F. Jones
1957	Evan A. Reiff

1958	W. Forbes Yarborough
1959-60	Ralph A. Phelps, Jr.
1960-62	Edwin F. Perry
1963-66	John A. Fincher
1967-68	John A. Southern

of the commission was worked out. Naturally these services were expanded and modified under Cornett's leadership. Later both Dr. Brantley and Dr. Fisher expanded and altered these objectives somewhat as circumstances demanded. Such change was both natural and desirable.

Up to this point we have spoken in general terms of the various projects and programs which the commission was promoting. Dr. Cornett laid out a general overall program which he followed. In an article written for the *Encyclopedia of Southern Baptists* not long before he left the commission he summarized these various projects as they were followed during his administration. We can do no better than to quote his statements of these:

The work of the Commission may be presented under five headings:

1. Stimulating and promoting a sympathetic interest in Christian Education. This was done through: (A) producing of articles and features for Baptist publications, (B) publication of *The Southern Baptist Educator, Southern Baptist Career News* (now *College and Career**), the *Southern Baptist Campus Directory,* and numerous tracts, (C) organizing general promotional efforts for Christian higher education, and (D) annual reports to the Convention.

---

* This publication was later turned over to the Sunday School Board.

43

2. Service to specific schools, done in several ways, including (A) faculty placement bureau, and (B) surveys and conferences on peculiar problems which certain institutions have.

3. Service to organized Baptist groups, done by conducting surveys for state conventions, boards of trustees, and so on. The Commission furnishes counsel for states or cities which contemplate starting a college.

4. Promoting cooperative enterprises among the various Baptist schools.

5. The promotion of a coordinated program of vocational guidance for Baptist young people.

Perhaps the most widespread, popular, and effective enterprise developed and promoted by the commission has been the annual Convention-wide emphasis on Christian education, at first in April, and later changed to the third Sunday in February. This program was begun in 1954 and has continued to be a big and impressive undertaking. The annual emphasis for the years 1954-1956 "resulted in features, articles, lessons and programs in more than a score of Convention-wide periodicals with combined circulation in excess of four million, and wide coverage in the Baptist state papers reaching more than a million Baptist homes." The number of tracts and leaflets on Christian higher education produced and distributed totals several million. This education emphasis in all the states of the Convention has brought the Baptist colleges to the attention of thousands of Baptist families.

The Sunday School Board, through its various departments with literally millions of readers, has been most generous in its cooperation, While this board in the nature of the case was able to give such valuable assistance, it should be said that some other boards and agencies of the Convention have also given encouragement and assistance in many ways.

Dr. Cornett feels that one of the most important phases of the commission's work during his tenure in office was the conducting of surveys at the request of the state Baptist conventions, executive boards, committees and associations. Dr. Cornett directed several such surveys, fulfilling requests from Kentucky (1951),

44

Texas (1952), Louisville (1956), and South Carolina (1958). He led in the study of the capital needs of Baptist schools in Georgia (1954) and Missouri (1955). The commission assisted in working out a formula in several states for dividing Christian education funds among the Baptist schools of those states.

During his eight years as executive secretary-treasurer, Cornett

Commissioner for Higher Education in the education office of the Department of Health, Education and Welfare, and later became director of that organization's Division of Educational Organization and Administration. He serves now as director of Cued Speech Program for Gallaudet College for the Deaf.

The resignation of Dr. Cornett made it necessary for the commission to begin the search for a new executive secretary-treasurer. During the seven months before the new official could be found and installed, Dr. Ralph A. Phelps, Jr., president of Ouachita Baptist College and chairman of the commission at the time, served in both capacities.

The work of the search committee of the commission ended with recommendation of Dr. Rabun Brantley as the executive secretary-treasurer in August of 1959.

Dr. Brantley is a native of Sylvania, Georgia, and a graduate of Mercer University. He was awarded the Ph.D. degree by George Peabody College for Teachers. In 1945 he became president of Virginia Intermont College in Bristol, Virginia, where he served until he was elected vice-president of Mercer University in July, 1956. From this position he came to the commission in September, 1959. With a fine family background, a wide acquaintance with educators, and valuable experience as an educator he was ready to devote his energies to the challenges offered by the commission.

Naturally, Dr. Brantley himself is more conversant with what was done during his term as executive secretary than any one else, so we asked him to furnish us a brief resume of these achievements. With understandable reluctance he agreed to do this, so we are quoting his statements verbatim. He speaks modestly in this account.

Some things we have been able to do since I came in 1959 are as follows:

1. Continue and expand the well begun emphasis in the churches on Christian education and Baptist schools when the commission prepares annual materials to be sold to the churches planning to hold an emphasis for intermediates and young people. This emphasis is designed to call attention to the advantages of the Baptist colleges to young people, and also to help them decide on a college and a proper career.

2. Moving Baptist College and Seminary Sunday from April to the third Sunday in February and establishing the day indefinitely on the third Sunday every year.

3. Expansion of exhibits for conferences and conventions. Furnishing pickup tracts at Ridgecrest, Glorieta, and other places.

4. Taking over from the Executive Committee the administration of the Dorothea Van Deusen Opdyke scholarship fund. More than 125 awards are made annually to students at 45 schools. The corpus of the fund is $250,000, and only the interest is used for student aid.

5. Through cooperation of the Southern Baptist Foundation and the Southern Baptist Convention Executive Committee, the commission administers the income from the Robertson-Sheppard fund and the J. W. Farmer fund. Loans are made to graduate students above the M.A. degree who are studying for the doctorate. The loans may be repaid at the rate of $750 a year for teaching in a Baptist school

after receiving the doctorate, or in cash plus interest in case the teacher goes with a non-Baptist school.

6. Sponsoring what was for the staff the three-year (1965-1967) Baptist Education Study Task (BEST), which involved over 8,000 Southern Baptists and was declared to be the most far-reaching effort ever made by Southern Baptists in higher edu-

8. Began participating in 1965 as one of the ten denominations in the Cooperative College Registry, thus adding several thousand additional names to the files of available teachers.

9. Began circulation in 1967 of a weekly column for Baptist papers entitled "Education: What's Happening." Improved coverage of all educational and college news.

10. Changed name of *Career News* to *College and Career,* used by some colleges as a recruitment mailing piece. Letters of appreciation for the contents of *College and Career* come from all over the country. Ten issues are published a year. It is mass-mailed to teenagers by many churches.

11. Baptist schools began paying some of their annual dues to *The Southern Baptist Educator* in order to have the paper sent to all faculty and trustees. Circulation increased to about 7,000 for the nine issues annually. Annual payment is now $2,300 from the Association which helps substantially in the total cost.

These are some of the main things that I think of. Maybe others are worthy of mention.

47

These modest statements naturally do not give an adequate account of what occurred during the eleven years of Dr. Brantley's administration. For example, the biggest event, the Baptist Education Study Task (BEST) had not been completed when he made these statements. This big project will be considered a bit later. Furthermore, the routine functions of the office now well established were carried on faithfully; new duties were taken on, and the office staff was enlarged to discharge these added responsibilities. It was during his administration (1962) that the commission headquarters were moved to the new Southern Baptist Convention building in Nashville.

Without question the most significant event during the eleven years of Dr. Brantley's administration was the conceiving, planning and execution of the Baptist Education Study Task (BEST). In fact this project has come to be recognized by Baptist educators as, at that time, the most comprehensive study ever undertaken by the Education Commission. Few, if any, denominations have engaged in a venture so exhaustive in scope, so thorough in execution, and so complete in its "wrap up." The study covered over two years, involved more than 8,000 competent people, and included 24 seminars and two national conferences.

Obviously, it is impossible here to deal adequately with this study. Indeed, Dr. Brantley, who served as general chairman, in writing the final report produced a book of over a hundred pages. For our purpose here it seems advisable to quote certain pertinent paragraphs from Dr. Brantley's complete report, thereby letting him speak directly to the reader.

> On January 22, 1965, an informal group of 15 persons met in Nashville to discuss some of the baffling problems facing Southern Baptists in the operation of their colleges in the 16 states where schools are located. There were three presidents of Baptist colleges, two deans, six denominational workers, two pastors, a Baptist administrative vice-president of a non-Baptist college, and a Baptist professor in a non-Baptist university.
>
> Agreeing that something needed to be done for the colleges, the group decided to ask the Education Commission of the Southern Baptist Convention to sponsor a two-year study and seek financial assistance from the

Executive Committee of the Southern Baptist Convention. The study would be concluded in 1967, the year Southern Baptists would emphasize "The Church Fulfilling Its Mission Through Education."

At its semiannual meeting in February, 1965, the Executive Committee approved an appropriation of $25,000 from the Convention operating reserve fund

retary, Executive Committee, S.B.C., Nashville, Tennessee, Chairman; E. N. Jones, secretary, Christian Education Commission, Baptist General Convention of Texas, Dallas, Texas, Vice-Chairman; and Marjorie Howard, administrative assistant, Education Commission, S.B.C., Nashville, Tennessee, Secretary.

To resume quotation from the publication entitled Baptist Education Study Task:

A second allocation of $25,000 was made by the Executive Committee for 1967.

The purposes of the study task were stated as follows:

to identify and study the issues, problems, and opportunities facing Southern Baptist higher education.

to explore these issues and problems in the context of current American higher education and of the needs and objectives of the denomination.

to consolidate findings and suggest a reasonable basis on which Southern Baptist higher education may advance.

In proceeding with the study, the Steering Committee sought to accumulate and evaluate basic information needed for a general study of the higher education situation in the Southern Baptist Convention. This information was then disseminated by means of study seminars, church and college groups, planned diffusion, and comprehensive publicity.

The two national study conferences were designed to inform Baptist leaders of the issues prevailing in their colleges, to involve Baptist leaders in discussions of the issues and problems, and to prepare a summary paper setting forth the facts, issues, and possible solutions for the purpose of review during the ensuing year by churches, pastors' conferences, and special groups. The second conference especially sought to refine the report in the hope that it would set forth a workable basis on which Southern Baptist higher education may be conducted in the future.

The study was called Baptist Education Study Task, or familiarly, BEST. It sought to be a systematic appraisal of the future role of Southern Baptists in Christian higher education. Twenty-four seminars of about 20 persons each were set up in 17 states having Baptist colleges, or planning one. The seminars met three times over a three-month period in the spring of 1966, and three more times in the spring of 1967, totaling 18 or more hours each. The First National Conference of 300 persons was held in Nashville on June 13-16, 1966, and the Second National Conference of approximately 300 persons was held in Nashville on June 12-15, 1967.

In determining the persons to be invited to participate in the seminars and national conferences, the utmost care was taken to provide as much balance as possible. State executive secretaries of Baptist conventions were asked to suggest names of persons interested in and knowledgeable about Christian higher education. The 54 college presidents were also asked to suggest trustees, pastors, students, and laymen to be invited. Hundreds of names were suggested and the Steering Committee worked from the top of the lists until a sufficient number had accepted. All presidents and deans were invited to the conferences but not in all cases to the seminars. Half of the colleges were asked to send their business managers and half were invited to send a faculty representative.

From the start, it was decided to limit the study to the 54 colleges, 39 of them senior and 15 of them junior. The seminaries, Bible schools, preparatory schools, and the program of student ministries (Baptist Student Union) were omitted, not that a sudy of them would have been unprofitable, but be-

50

cause these would have added to a diversity of problems already too great for proper treatment. Representatives from these institutions and programs were invited to participate in the conferences.

More than 8,000 persons participated in one or more areas of the study. Many of these were in pastors' conferences, college faculties, and adult study groups in churches over a wide

1. Biblical Basis for Christian Higher Education
2. A Brief History of Southern Baptist Higher Education
3. American Higher Education 1958-68
4. Relation of Southern Baptist Higher Education to American Higher Education
5. College-Denominational Relationships
6. Financing Christian Higher Education
7. Academic Freedom and Responsibility
8. The Christian College Teacher
9. Religious Scope of Christian Higher Education
10. Academic Scope of Christian Higher Education
11. Preface to a Philosophy of Christian Higher Education
12. Accreditation

The following quotation of the summary statement from the book on BEST, published in 1967 by the Education Commission, should make clear the significance of the study:

> The Baptist Education Study Task has made it possible for approximately 8,000 interested Baptists from a number of states to study and discuss formally over a period of two years the major aspects

of Christian higher education as they relate to Baptist colleges and universities.

Current problems were defined and pertinent data analyzed. Issues were identified and discussed in relation to apparent underlying causes, and possible means were suggested for their resolution.

Free and frank discussion was engaged in with full recognition that this was a study task and that no official actions by the participants were contemplated. Differences of opinion were expressed in a spirit of frankness and Christian forbearance.

Among the many significant outcomes of the Study, in addition to reports that have been presented covering the major areas of interest, are:

1. an increasing awareness of the significance of Christian higher education as an integral component of the Baptist witness.

2. a more enlightened understanding of the present difficulties that confront our Baptist colleges and universities.

3. a consciousness of need for definition of the purposes of Christian higher institutions in our present day culture, and for more effective relationship between the colleges and the denomination.

4. a more precise understanding of the nature and extent of financial support necessary to provide Christian higher education of acceptable quality.

5. a deeper understanding of the vital relationships between the colleges and the conventions that foster and support them, and a clearer understanding of the areas of control and lines of responsibility.

6. a rededication on the part of many to the improvement and strengthening of the Baptist colleges and universities.

It may not be repetitious to close this discussion of BEST by quoting the thoughtful and forceful analysis of the project by Dr. Ben C. Fisher in *The Southern Baptist Educator* (November-December, 1973):

BAPTIST EDUCATION STUDY TASK

The Baptist Education Study Task, completed in 1968, represents the most thorough study that Southern Baptists have ever made of their colleges and the relationship of these institutions to the denomination. This study has had, and continues to have, a profound influence on the direction of Baptist higher education.

the major achievements will be identified.

In the first place, at the time when this study was undertaken, Southern Baptist colleges were running into grave difficulties with the College Delegate Assembly of the Southern Association of Colleges and Schools concerning accreditation. The problem in the main centered around the general lack of understanding on the part of Baptist leadership of both the process of, and the necessity for, accreditation; and an equal lack of understanding on the part of the accrediting agency as to the nature of Baptist polity. What was almost certainly a collision course on the matter of institutional control and the election of Baptist trustees was avoided, although a complete solution to this problem has not yet been reached. The opening of new channels of communication between the colleges and the denomination and between the denomination and the accrediting agencies was one of the most significant accomplishments of this study.

In the second place, the Baptist Education Study Task called attention to the importance of each institution's developing a forthright and honest statement of Christian purpose, and structuring guidelines for achieving these goals. Since the first, and in many ways the prime, standard of the accrediting agency is *purpose,* this contribution becomes doubly important.

In the third place, the Baptist Education Study Task report contributed immeasurably to trustee orientation, particularly in the area of denominational relations. As a result of this study, an orientation manual for college trustees was produced, and the third edition has been nearly sold out. In addition, annual state, regional, and institutional conferences have been set up.

In the fourth place, the Baptist Education Study Task identified major problems in denominational relations and offered guidelines toward reaching solutions. These have been put to good use in administrative conferences, faculty workshops, forums, and seminars for pastors and denominational leaders, and in many other areas.

In the fifth place, the Baptist Education Study Task provided a forum in which one of the most touchy and potentially divisive issues ever to arise in the Southern Baptist Convention was thoroughly debated. The matter of federal and state aid to Baptist colleges and schools had aroused a bitter and sometimes raucous debate. Since this time, while feelings on both sides remain strong, there has been less acrimony and more reasoned dialogue.

Sixth, and in many ways most important, a fresh understanding was reached as to the necessity of having each Baptist college attain a thorough understanding of the theological and Biblical presuppositions on which Christian higher education rests.

In accepting the report of the committee, the Convention in 1968 approved this significant statement: "In view of the commitment by Baptists to promote the Christian message through effective witnessing, Christian education is not an optional interest of the church, but an important function of its mission. Baptists have established and they continue to support colleges because the colleges share with the church in the ultimate purpose of the redemptive plan of God for mankind.

"Because no effective substitute has been found for the genuinely Christian college, Baptists must continue to nurture and support adequately their Christian institutions of higher education."

One member with several years' experience on the commission recently said to this writer: "Dr. Brantley was a trained journalist who knew how to write. He worked quietly and calmly. He was cool in a crisis; he did not panic. He could be patient. These qualities were just what was needed at this time."

CHAPTER VI

The retirement of Secretary Brantley in 1970 marked the end of approximately twenty years of the Education Commission under the leadership of the first two executive secretaries. In a sense this may be regarded as the end of an era. Even a hurried look at the situation in 1970 will show that this was a crucial time.

The commission was now well established in the minds of Baptists and was enjoying a high degree of public favor. The Baptist Education Study Task had been completed. The stimulus created by this big venture was being felt. It was highly desirable that this momentum be maintained. Several urgent recommendations coming out of BEST needed now to be undertaken.

One of these was to project a national colloquium on Christian higher education, which would require a tremendous amount of careful planning by skillful leaders in education. The colloquium was envisioned as a critical examination of the nature, the purpose, and the program of a genuine Christian college.

There was a growing conviction among Baptists that there should be a much more vital and workable relationship between Baptist colleges and schools and the agencies of the Southern Baptist Convention, especially the Foreign Mission Board, the Home Mission Board, and the Woman's Missionary Union, partly because the colleges furnish such a big percentage of the personnel of these mission organizations. Indeed, the leaders of twenty years from now, in all areas of mission work, are students now on the campuses of Baptist schools. It seemed to many that it would be advantageous for mission agencies to have much closer contact with these students, and that it would be to the advantage of mission-minded students to be involved with these boards as early as possible. College leaders themselves felt that they also would benefit greatly in such an arrangement. It became evident that to develop these plans would require strong leadership. To lead out in this project has become the responsibility of the Education Commission.

Every student of missions knows that on the mission field one of the first and most vital steps is to establish a school. As a consequence, there are now many schools on mission fields. Some of these are well-established colleges doing excellent work. Recently there had been suggestions that the commission could be helpful to these overseas schools in various ways. Here was an inviting opportunity to establish a working arrangement that could be advantageous to colleges at home and to mission schools abroad.

Up to this time little had been done either by the schools themselves or by the commission to provide instruction and inspiration to the trustees of the various schools. Here was another field of service.

Perhaps the one idea most prominent in the minds of Baptists at the time was the conviction that the time had come for their colleges to examine themselves with the purpose of becoming genuine Christian schools. The Christian college is an institution unique to this country. It has a history; it has a mission. Without apology, Baptists feel that such a college should strive to be Christian, and to emphasize Christian values which make a difference in the quality of life of the student.

All of these and perhaps other significant issues had to be faced by the commission in 1970. The big question was, "Who will now become the leader of the Education Commission?"

The chairman of the committee to nominate the next executive director-treasurer was President William K. Weaver, Jr., of Mobile College. The committee took seriously its responsibility, which demanded heavy correspondence and frequent conferences. Naturally the group received recommendations from various interested persons, and considered each one carefully. As the work proceeded,

the committee was becoming convinced that the man best qualified for the position was then a member of the commission, was
indeed chairman of the commission. Having arrived at a hearty
decision, the committee offered the position to Dr. Ben C. Fisher.
However, Dr. Fisher felt that in his situation as chairman of
the commission it would not be wise to accept. A bit later the
committee renewed the offer to Dr. Fisher, who stated that he
was happy in his work as executive director of the Council

ated from Wake Forest College with the A.B. degree in 1938. An-
dover Newton Theological School awarded him the M.Div. degree
in 1942. He later did graduate work in the University of North
Carolina. He has two honorary degrees: LL.D. from Campbell
College, 1968, and D.D. from Wake Forest University in 1971. In
1940 he was married to Miss Sara Gehman of Ambler, Pennsyl-
vania, and they have two sons.

In Fisher's professional career he has held several responsible
positions. He served as pastor of four Baptist churches (1938-
1947). For five years he served in several capacities at Gardner-
Webb Junior College. He spent eight years at Southeastern Baptist
Theological Seminary as administrative assistant to the president,
as director of public relations, and as professor of Christian education. In 1962 he was elected executive director of the Council
on Christian Higher Education of the Baptist State Convention of
North Carolina.

During his years in North Carolina as he became a leader in
educational services, he was also active in civic affairs. One of the
activities in which he still takes particular pride was his service
on a special commission, appointed by Governor Dan K. Moore
of North Carolina, called the Commission on the Study of the
Statutes Relating to Visiting Speakers at State Supported Institutions. He was the only educator on this commission, which held
televised hearings and was able eventually to prevent public colleges and universities in North Carolina from losing their accred-

itation. The North Carolina General Assembly, in a hasty action, had placed such severe restrictions on those who could speak on a public university campus that the Southern Association of Colleges and Schools had served notice that unless the restrictions were lifted, all the public colleges and universities in North Carolina would lose their accreditation. In order to resolve the problem, it was necessary for the governor of North Carolina to call the legislature into a special session to enact the solution suggested by the special commission. Fisher and other members of the group received citations for their services.

During the latter years of Fisher's stay in North Carolina he served as a consultant to the state of North Carolina's Board of Higher Education, and in that capacity he prepared for publication a monograph and bibliography on *Duties and Responsibilities of College and University Trustees,* and contributed to the preparation of the section on governance entitled "Institutional Policy and Administration," Chapter V in the definitive study called *Planning for Higher Education in North Carolina,* published in 1968.

Fisher also was active in organizing the North Carolina Association of Independent Colleges, and became its first director during 1969 and 1970.

In 1966 he became a member of the Education Commission of the Southern Baptist Convention and served as chairman of the commission from 1968 to 1970. Dr. Fisher is a prolific writer. He has served as editor of several educational journals and has written scores of articles on Christian education and several books in the field of higher education. He is in demand as a public speaker on many occasions. He has traveled widely, visiting several overseas countries in the interest of Christian education. When he became a member of the commission in 1966, he was already recognized as an authority in the field of Christian higher education.

As the new leader assumed the duties of his office, it seems appropriate to tell something about those who were to work with him in what appeared to be a new era in commission history.

As we have mentioned previously, at the time Dr. Fisher became executive director-treasurer of the commission, one matter of great concern was the development of a closer working relation between the Baptist schools and the agencies of the Southern Baptist Convention. Dr. Fisher heartily favored this improved denominational relationship, but was aware of the size of the undertaking. With the ever-growing responsibilities of the commission he felt that it would be necessary to employ another person to assume these special responsibilities. In his search, he became convinced that a man then serving as a member of the commission was ideally

versity, Auburn, Alabama, in 1950. He served in the U. S. Navy from 1944 to 1946 and in the U. S. Air Force from 1951 to 1952. After graduation from the university he worked successfully as a civil engineer, but could not resist the ever-growing conviction that he should enter the ministry. To prepare for this work he entered New Orleans Baptist Theological Seminary where he was awarded the B.D. degree in 1956. He served as pastor in Fordoche, Louisiana, for three years. Then he became pastor of the First Baptist Church in Parsons, Tennessee, 1956-1961. His next pastorate was in the First Baptist Church at Cookeville, Tennessee, from 1961 to 1975.

He was active in denominational work as a member of the executive board of the Tennessee Baptist Convention for several years, and as president of this board for two years; he served as vice-president of the Tennessee convention one year and president of the pastors' conference one year. He was a member of the board of trustees of Baptist Hospital in Nashville for nine years.

Dr. Capps was married to Miss Betty Tipler of Grand Junction, Tennessee, in 1953. He and Mrs. Capps are the parents of two sons and one daughter.

As stated above, he came to the commission as director of denominational relations. His work in all areas has been so satisfactory that the commission recently elected him Associate Executive Director.

61

Some twenty-four years ago there came to the office of the commission a young lady to begin her work as a typist. Little did she or any member of the commission dream that she was beginning a remarkable career of service to hundreds of Southern Baptist educators, to thousands of students, to countless teachers and pastors. This young lady was Miss Marjorie Howard, who was living with her mother in Nashville. She was a student in George Peabody College for Teachers in Nashville.

She proved to be an efficient typist and secretary. Her competence was enhanced by her cheerful disposition, her friendly manner, and her sincere purpose to serve. She soon became secretary to the two executive secretaries, first to Dr. Cornett and then to Dr. Brantley. A bit later she was asked to become administrative assistant. Recently she was made Director of Administrative Services of the Education Commission. We are told that she is the first woman in any Southern Baptist agency to direct a division of work. One can easily imagine the value of her services after almost a quarter century of continuous work in the offices of the Education Commission.

Two other ladies, each of whom has given almost twenty years of service in the commission offices, are Mrs. Lela Beal (now retired) and Mrs. Jeanne Cathey. Such services are usually in the background and are not properly recognized. In this case, all three executive directors, Cornett, Brantley and Fisher, have expressed great appreciation to these staff members for their contributions to the work of the commission.

In 1966 Mr. W. Howard Bramlette, who had spent several years in the Student Department of the Sunday School Board, came to the commission as Director of Placement and Promotion. His experience of several years in denominational work and his interest in young people were to his advantage, but he later decided to accept an invitation to return to the Student Department of the Sunday School Board, where he now serves as design editor of student materials.

The latest addition to the staff of the commission is Dr. Howard G. Kirksey, who recently was elected as Placement Consultant. His department has grown rapidly, and is such an important part of the program of the commission that a professional director is needed.

Dr. Kirksey received his A.B. degree from Union University and his M.A. and Ph.D. degrees from George Peabody College. He has served widely in Baptist denominational affairs, and is retired from his former position as vice-president for academic affairs at Middle Tennessee State University, Murfreesboro, Tennessee. His activities in the field of higher education have won many honors. He serves on a part-time basis.

to improve their academic standards; to challenge Southern Baptists to place their entire national resources behind their educational institutions in student recruitment, in alumni support, and in individual, corporate, and foundation giving; and to project Southern Baptist educational institutions as national assets, both to the denomination and to the republic.

Dr. Fisher had the advantage of several years' experience as a member of the commission. Another advantage he enjoyed was the fact that a special self-study committee of the commission had just completed its final report, and the benefits of this study were available to the new executive director-treasurer. Naturally the new leader had plans which would involve some changes, but he was wise enough to move slowly. He was particularly concerned that every member of the staff should be treated with fairness. He was deeply appreciative of the work already done by the commission and was convinced that most of the established programs should be continued.

In his first official report to the Convention in June, 1971, he gave his hearty endorsement to the conclusions reached by the self-study committee as follows:

> The self-study committee concluded that the basis
> for the continuation of our Baptist witness in high-
> er education includes a determination on the part of
> the individual institutions to live within stated Chris-

tian purposes, the willingness of these institutions to serve the denomination in vital relationships, and the willingness (even while limiting enrollments and expansion of facilities) to strive constantly for academic excellence.

In addition to the traditional services which our Baptist colleges render to our denomination and to our people, these institutions have given strong moral leadership in an age of moral decline. They have refused to bow to the popular dictum that a college has no responsibility for student conduct. They have refused to allow radical minorities, either in the student body or faculty, to take over or disrupt the orderly process of instruction. While championing academic freedom and the right to peaceful assembly, Baptist colleges have not allowed the substitution of violence for the power of persuasion nor permitted anarchy in the guise of dissent or civil disobedience. To this extent they have served not only their denomination but all of higher education in this country.

The Baptist Education Study Task identified as a major problem that of denominational relations and communication. The current crisis in higher education has caused our educational institutions to realize more fully the importance of Baptist support and the opportunity to assert their uniqueness particularly in statement of Christian purpose and commitment.

Church-related colleges are the last live option for post-high school training in a Christian atmosphere. At these colleges Christian codes of conduct are expected and these expectations are stated in writing. Christian standards are never more perfectly achieved on the campus than they are in the local church. However, the witness is present in both precept and example.

Christian colleges continue to make a vital contribution in the training of both church-related vocational workers and lay leadership.

To an extent which perhaps he himself did not anticipate at the time, these classic statements have proved to be an expression of the aim and objective of Dr. Fisher's administration.

Dr. Fisher was gratified at the greatly increased number of calls which were coming from the agencies of the Convention and from the schools themselves. They were asking for assistance in many areas, such as trustee orientation, accreditation, institutional self

Fisher's book, *An Orientation Manual for College Trustees,* first published in 1968, is now moving into its fourth edition. The manual has had wide distribution among other church-related groups as well as Baptists, and is often used by state-supported schools as well. A number of states in the convention were asking for trustee orientation conferences. These calls were answered as far as possible both on a state and institutional level.

In 1972-73 the commission sponsored a national conference in Nashville to discuss the role of the trustee in denominational affairs. This type of service by the commission was to increase year by year.

In various ways plans were being made to assist black colleges and schools. Since 1970, Fisher has served as a member of the United Board for College Development, a cooperative effort of all major denominations to assist in the development of black church-related colleges, particularly in securing funds and offering consultative services. In 1970, Dr. Fisher was asked by Dr. Porter Routh, executive secretary-treasurer of the Executive Committee of the Southern Baptist Convention, to provide consultative services to the Commission on the American Baptist Theological Seminary, an institution for black students in Nashville. This work has continued throughout Fisher's administration.

The improvements made in the make-up and the content of *The Southern Baptist Educator* have brought a steady increase in its circulation. This increase has continued so that in 1977 more than 10,000 copies of each issue are now published.

For several years the commission had emphasized the necessity of having Baptist colleges fully accredited. In 1972 the executive director-treasurer was able to announce that for the first time in history all Baptist colleges were fully accredited. All Southern Baptist seminaries had increased in enrollment, and the colleges showed an increase of some 5,000 students over the previous year. As a result of more vigorous efforts the Convention-wide emphasis for Baptist Seminary, College, and School Day for 1972 had been the best ever observed.

Dr. Fisher's vision was shown by a national student admissions workshop, with more than 80 college and seminary personnel involved, and a workshop for state education chairmen, both of which meetings were so successful in 1972 that they are now annual events. The placement bureau assisted 47 colleges in securing faculty members for 1972-73.

In 1973 a new area of service opened when a request came from the Hong Kong-Macao Baptist Mission, Hong Kong Baptist College, and the Foreign Mission Board for a special on-campus study of Hong Kong Baptist College. Dr. Fisher was authorized to make this study. On the same overseas mission he made an on-campus study of Seinan Gakuin University in Fukuoka, Japan. This proved to be a worthwhile experience which later led to published reports and another visit to both schools at the request of the Foreign Mission Board.

Dr. Fisher took three educational specialists with him on this second visit: Dr. Gordon Sweet, executive secretary, Commission on Colleges, Southern Association of Colleges and Schools; Dr. Daniel R. Grant, president of Ouachita Baptist University; and Dr. John E. Johns, then president of Stetson University. The conclusion reached, and published in printed reports on Hong Kong Baptist College and Seinan Gakuin University, was that the educational standards of these institutions are equal to, or exceed, the minimum requirements for accreditation in any regional accrediting agency within the United States. This informal statement has greatly facilitated both faculty and student exchange with Baptist institutions in this country, and also admission of students from these institutions to both public and private universities in America.

Dr. Fisher, at the request of President Penrose St. Amant of the Baptist Theological Seminary in Ruschlikon, Switzerland, and with the approval of the Foreign Mission Board, made a study of that school late in 1975, publishing the results in *The Southern Baptist Educator* early in 1976.

The extent of growth in the commission activities can be appreciated when one realizes that such special services as those

had selected Dr. George E. Capps, Jr., to serve as director of denominational relations for the commission.

Since Dr. Capps had had several years' experience as a member of the commission, and had served in many areas of denominational work, he was well oriented in his new responsibilities. In his work he has had occasion to fill many speaking engagements for the commission, and calls have been steadily increasing for workshops, seminars, surveys and special studies. To respond to these calls is not simply a matter of presiding at a conference; it requires a tremendous amount of "homework" in preparation for each occasion. As Dr. Fisher's duties became heavier, much of this "homework" fell to Dr. Capps.

In denominational relations, naturally, heavy correspondence is involved. Both Dr. Fisher and Dr. Capps deal with individual churches, district associations, state conventions, colleges and schools, and the various agencies of the Southern Baptist Convention. The Sunday School Board in many ways has cooperated with the commission. Frequently officials of this board have assisted by giving generous space in their various publications to different projects of the commission. They have been appreciative of assistance by the commission in many phases of their work. The Seminary Extension Department and the Education Commission have worked together on several projects.

In a special way the Foreign Mission Board, the Home Mission

Board and Woman's Missionary Union have been interested in the program of the Education Commission for years. Baptist college involvement in missions has been consistent since the founding of the first Baptist college. However, in June, 1974, upon the recommendation of the Education Commission, the Association of Southern Baptist Colleges and Schools recommitted itself to the cause of missions at home and abroad. Baptist college presidents took significant action when they voted unanimously to make missions not just a traditional campus committee assignment, but a matter of broad institutional policy involving administration, faculty, students, trustees, and alumni.

There followed meetings of the Baptist college presidents with Dr. Baker James Cauthen and his staff from the Foreign Mission Board in Richmond, Dr. William G. Tanner and his staff of the Home Mission Board in Atlanta, and Miss Carolyn Weatherford, head of Woman's Missionary Union and her staff in Birmingham.

Two resulting resolutions indicate the ways in which these agencies continue to work together:

FOREIGN MISSION BOARD RESOLUTION ON CHRISTIAN EDUCATION

WHEREAS the Education Commission of the Southern Baptist Convention and the Association of Southern Baptist Colleges and Schools in June, 1974, in Pineville, Louisiana, reaffirmed the commitment of Baptist higher education to the worldwide missionary enterprise of Southern Baptists, and

WHEREAS there has been for over one hundred and fifty years a vital relationship between world missions and our Baptist institutions of higher education in this country; and

WHEREAS Baptist colleges, universities, seminaries, and other schools continue to contribute greatly to world missions in the recruitment and training of missionaries, and in other important ways;

BE IT THEREFORE RESOLVED that the Foreign Mission Board of the Southern Baptist Convention, meeting in Ridgecrest, North Carolina, on July 3, 1974:

1. Expresses deep gratitude for the past and present support of world missions by Baptist schools;

2. Reaffirms the essential role of Baptist higher education in the world missionary enterprise;

3. Rejoices in the prospect of increased missionary emphasis

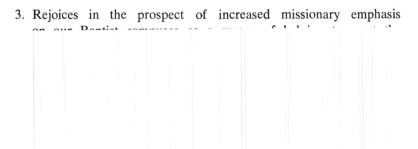

stitutions of the Association, in their renewed efforts to undergird a new concern for world missions on the campuses of Baptist schools.

HOME MISSION BOARD RESOLUTION
ON CHRISTIAN EDUCATION

It is recommended that the following resolution be adopted:

RECOGNIZING the vital role of the Education Commission of the Southern Baptist Convention and the Association of Southern Baptist Colleges and Schools in the recruitment and training of home mission personnel, and the creating of mission awareness of all students, faculty and staff;

BE IT THEREFORE RESOLVED that the Home Mission Board of the Southern Baptist Convention, Atlanta, Georgia, July 20, 1977:

1. Expresses sincere appreciation for the continual participation of Baptist schools in home missions through the integration of the learning laboratory and the mission experience; and

2. Rejoices in the privilege of giving special recognition to students from Baptist colleges who participate in home missions; of creating special home mission opportunities for Baptist col-

leges; and of sharing with churches the contribution of Baptist colleges to home missions; and

3. Commits personnel, material and other resources to Baptist colleges for the interpretation of home mission concepts, the recruitment of home mission personnel and the promotion of home mission programs; and

4. Pledges a more vital working relationship with the Education Commission of the Southern Baptist Convention and the Association of Southern Baptist Colleges and Schools.

The two mission boards have shown a most enthusiastic response. Lengthy conferences with leaders of both boards have revealed two facts: (1) the eagerness of the boards to cooperate heartily and (2) the large number of possibilities in areas of service which heretofore had not been realized. Plans are now being made to involve a larger number of students in summer programs at home and overseas. Other campus activities and special programs are being planned which will challenge students. Missions will be a subject for discussion in faculty and trustee workshops. All of these plans hold great promise both for the schools and for the mission boards.

This brief report of denominational activities of the commission under the leadership of Dr. Fisher will show how conscientiously the commission is endeavoring to carry out the recommendations made by the Baptist Education Study Task.

While all these denominational matters are important, it must be remembered that the business of a college is to function in the field of higher education. Southern Baptist schools must be first grade academically. To do this, they must keep in touch with educational agencies. Dr. Fisher has served as liaison between Baptist colleges and such organizations as the Council for the Advancement of Small Colleges, the Association of Governing Boards of Universities and Colleges, the American Alumni Council, American Association of Higher Education, The Association of American Colleges, the National Association of Independent Colleges and Universities, and several others. Such participation requires time and travel, but it is necessary—as is the effort to keep in touch with other Christian bodies who maintain church-related colleges.

Another area of service which has grown rapidly in recent years is "keeping in touch with Washington." As the federal government expands its interest in higher education, the welfare of any college may be involved in national legislation at almost any time. This means that the director of the commission must be in Washington several times a year. This is a delicate and difficult mission but one that should not be neglected at this time.

CHAPTER VII

The first three years of Dr. Fisher's administration were exceedingly busy ones. Each year had presented new opportunities for commission action, and the director had been eager to accept these new challenges. Much had been achieved, and still new areas of service opened up with regularity. However, by 1973 the one big project which was commanding the attention of the commission was the National Colloquium. Month by month its significance and its possibilities grew. It was now considered not simply a desirable venture but a matter of necessity. The times called for it.

A bit later we shall consider the situation which called for such a conference. In 1972 the Association of Southern Baptist Colleges and Schools voted unanimously to request the Education Commission to sponsor a national colloquium to deal constructively with issues and challenges in contemporary church-related education. In its meeting in June, 1973, the commission voted heartily to endorse the idea and proceed with plans.

Naturally certain committees would be needed. The one committee which would have to make the big decisions was the Steering Committee. After long and careful discussion the following men were selected for this committee:

Abner V. McCall, Chairman

George E. Bagley

Chester Brown

John A. Fincher

E. Harold Fisher

Daniel R. Grant

E. Bruce Heilman

H. I. Hester

Robert L. Lynn

James L. Sells

Budd E. Smith

William G. Tanner

Ruric E. Wheeler

Dr. Fisher and Dr. Capps met regularly with the committee. Meetings were held when necessary, even up to the time of the colloquium. Coming out of these meetings were the decisions as to the time, place, purpose, and program personnel.

For obvious reasons, it was heartily agreed to have this conference in 1976, the Bicentennial year of the nation. The ideal time was in June, just prior to the meeting of the Southern Baptist Convention in Norfolk, Virginia. Therefore the colloquium was planned to take the place of the annual meeting of the Association of Southern Baptist Colleges and Schools (usually held in June). In order that it might take place in "historic territory," Williamsburg, Virginia, was selected as the site. The meetings were held in the Phi Beta Kappa auditorium of William and Mary College, founded in 1693, one of the oldest church-related colleges in the United States. The purpose was of extraordinary significance. This program was not to deal with any one of the dozen or more topics usually considered at such meetings. It was to consider the very reason for the existence of a Christian school. With this objective in mind, the very best speakers and leaders available were to be secured.

We go back now to consider the reasons for undertaking this big venture. Why expend the time and the effort of so many people in a meeting of four days? One of the hearty recommendations of the Baptist Education Study Task (BEST) of 1967 was that periodically a national colloquium ought to be held on Southern Baptist higher education. As Dr. Fisher and his colleagues became involved in this project, they were gripped by its possibilities. It was no longer a matter of carrying out a suggestion made by a study group; this was now a project which inspired the enthusiastic support of leaders in Southern Baptist higher education.

tions, which have given so much to the development of Southern Baptists and to the advancement of general education in our society.

In the year 1976, when the country as a whole will observe its two hundredth anniversary, the considerable contribution of Southern Baptists should not go unnoticed. This is indeed a time for celebrating the past, rejoicing in the present, and facing the future with confidence.

These are not easy times for general education, public or private. We entered the seventies with severe erosion of public confidence, major conflicts in the Far and Middle East, deep-seated emotional turmoil over the Vietnam involvement, rapid development of the drug culture, rebellion of an alienated youth, campus rioting (along with a senseless destruction of property), and the involvement of some faculty and students in radical social reform. Baptists were most fortunate. Major confrontations were avoided largely because Baptist colleges were among the first to structure student participation in institutional governance.

More recently, we have been confronted in the public secondary schools with severe money shortages, teachers' strikes, and recalcitrant state general assemblies which have decreased appropriations, in some cases punitively.

In addition, the aftermath of Watergate has left the American public further confused and bewildered. Articles in several national magazines have pointed out that almost without exception, the Watergate principals are college and university graduates.

The basic purpose of general education is being seriously questioned. We have to admit that in public education from kindergarten through the university, the attempt to inculcate moral values and ethical principles to a large degree has either failed or been abandoned altogether.

However, there are hopeful signs, and among these are the many educators, public and private, who are calling for a rethinking of the university's responsibility for the transmission of values, and for assisting the student in developing his ability to make value judgments.

Moreover, there is evidence that among parents and students there is growing disenchantment with permissiveness and a new concern for morality and responsible citizenship.

Therefore, in this general climate Baptist schools have never had a greater opportunity, both to articulate and to communicate their basic Christian purpose. This is a time for reaffirming some fundamental Biblical and theological presuppositions. Among these reaffirmations should be a restatement of belief in a loving and unchanging God, revealed fully in Jesus Christ, as the basis for hope; the love of God and the love of neighbor as a basis for Christian ethics; and the Ten Commandments as trustworthy guides for human conduct.

The assumption that these truths are always self-evident is a tenuous one. Christians in all generations have found it necessary to examine these Christian absolutes within the context and needs of their own time.

The time is also right for a reexamination of Christianity and culture, particularly as the Christian community becomes more and more isolated by the rising tide of secularism. A fundamental question for

damage that a barren existential philosophy has done to the Christian concept of time in which only the present seems important? In this point of view the past has no real meaning and the future holds no hope since there is no belief in what Albert Outler once described as the three great deeds of God—Creation, Redemption, and Consummation. How can the Christian idea of liberal education be redeemed and once more made an effective instrument for projecting Christian values? These questions represent only a few of the broad areas being proposed for study over the next three-year period.

Another major objective of the colloquium is to produce a variety of materials that can be shared with Baptist pastors and other church leaders. We hope that these materials can be used as the bases for workshops, seminars, and regional meetings in which both pastors and laymen can be involved. The future of Baptist educational institutions to a large degree will depend upon their ability to communicate their purpose and to work in partnership with the local church.

Without attempting to comment on Dr. Fisher's statement we should like to remind the reader that its chief emphasis is on the fact that a school cannot be a really Christian institution without being Christian in its entire program and without being sustained by the hearty moral and financial support of a body of Christian people.

The general theme chosen for this four-day colloquium was "Looking to the Third Century with Confidence." A total of sixty men and women had part on the program. These were carefully selected as authorities in their field. While most of them are Baptists, several other leading denominations are represented.

Five general sessions were held, in each of which there were usually two special addresses. In each session the audience made certain positive reaffirmations which are included in this chapter. In addition to these formal sessions five special seminars and workshops were conducted, with the colloquium coming to a close at noon Saturday, June 12, 1976.

Perhaps the one feature of these sessions which won the approbation of all present was the "Reaffirmations," written by Dr. Ben C. Fisher and approved before the colloquium by the steering committee. These historic statements embodied the basic purpose of the entire conference. For this reason we are including these in this chapter.

The following reaffirmations have grown out of the major themes which have served as the guidelines in developing our National Colloquium.

These reaffirmations are offered only to serve as guidelines for individuals and institutions who wish to reexamine seriously the Christian basis for education and who wish to engage in a renewed commitment to the great Biblical and doctrinal themes which have guided in centuries past.

We also believe that these truths are a summons to all Baptists to enter into the third century in the life of this republic, in obedience to the Great Commission, firmly committed to an undiminished support of our historic emphasis on Missions, Evangelism, and Education.

REAFFIRMATIONS

Our Covenant Relationship

As we look to the third century with confidence, we reaffirm our allegiance to the covenant relationship between our churches and our schools, a covenant which finds its unity in the purpose of God, the mind of Christ, the work of the Spirit, and the

Unity in Diversity

We reaffirm the unity in diversity that has enabled Baptists to witness in faithfulness and creativity.

We reaffirm our gratitude for the historic support which Southern Baptists have given to their seminaries, colleges and schools.

We reaffirm our belief in, and support of, the Cooperative Program as the best instrument yet devised for the support of the complex work of our denomination.

We reaffirm our faith in, and support of, the local church, and the broad programs of our denomination.

Christian Witness in a Secular Culture

We reaffirm our belief that man is created by a loving and beneficent God. We reaffirm that man has both a transcendent origin and a transcendent destiny, and that he is ever the object of God's concern and redeeming love, through Christ Jesus, our Lord.

We further reaffirm our belief that the recurring crises in human affairs are the results of man's unwillingness, through pride and ignorance, to recognize either the nature or the extent of his sin; but believing as we do that God through Christ has intervened directly in the world and in the affairs of men for the salvation of his children, our schools and our churches confront the secular views of materialism and nihilism with the Christian message of faith, hope, and love, and with the Christian principle of the individual's infinite worth.

The Christian Idea of a Liberal Education

We reaffirm that Christian education rests upon the presupposition that all truth is of God. To believe in one true loving God means that there is an essential integrity in every dimension of human inquiry and in human experience. This is God's world, created, ordered, and sustained at his pleasure. Truth, we believe, never stands alone in any area, but is related to all truth, and always has the power to reveal the dynamic and creative grace of God.

We reaffirm that liberal arts studies have provided the context in which the Christian view of education can make its greatest impact. However, the earthen vessel of liberal arts education, unless also used to transmit the Biblical and theological content of the Christian faith, cannot effectively serve the church or its institutions.

We reaffirm that in a liberal arts education filled with such content, the implications of the Christian faith can be fully articulated to yield moral and intellectual excellence; develop responsible churchmen; produce active Christian citizens; create an attitude of tolerance and understanding; affirm the dignity and worth of the individual; defend civil, intellectual, and religious freedoms; and transmit the value system of Christian ethics.

Stewardship of Finance

We reaffirm the Biblical view of Christian stewardship that all persons, and all things, and all places belong to God, and that all things are to be used, and that all persons are to act, for His honor and glory.

We reaffirm that while persons may differ in their employment, they must all act for the same ends, as dutiful servants of God in the stewardship of their possessions and in the faithful performance of their several callings.

Christian Absolutes

We reaffirm our belief that there are Christian absolutes which history does not change nor time erode.

80

We reaffirm that in obedience to the clear teachings of Jesus Christ, we have a responsibility for helping to guide the student in the development of Christian character.

We reaffirm our belief that a central duty of Christian higher education is to transmit Christian ethical and moral values both by precept and example.

The Great Commission

We reaffirm our responsibility for carrying out the mandate of the Great Commission, at home and abroad, and for creating an atmosphere on our campuses in which young people can be made aware of, and challenged by, the opportunity for missionary service.

We further reaffirm our responsibility to work with our mission boards in recruiting and training missionaries, to assist Baptist educational institutions abroad with faculty-student exchanges and consultative services, to relate the study-abroad programs of Baptist schools where appropriate to foreign mission fields, and to develop special on-campus programs for missionary personnel on furlough.

We reaffirm also our commitment to develop in the laity a Christian world view that will be supportive of missions.

Student-Teacher Relationships

We reaffirm our responsibility to treat the student at all times as a person of worth; to instill in students a thirst for knowledge; to enable them to develop life goals; to help students to discriminate among values; and to encourage in them a Christian world view, responsible Christian citizenship, active participation in the life of their church, and the development of a sense of vocational mission.

We further reaffirm that it is our responsibility to lead students to a deeper commitment to Christ so that God's reconciling love may lead them to see that concern and involvement are the basis for the celebration of Christian faith.

We reaffirm our commitment to seek and employ the Christian teacher.

Stewardship of Management

We reaffirm our responsibility for the stewardship of management in every area of institutional operation.

We pledge ourselves to make the best use possible of all institutional resources and potentials committed to our care.

We reaffirm the management concept that is basically concerned with the development and welfare of the individual.

And we further reaffirm that all persons and all things in this world, since they truly belong to God, should be devoted to divine service, and that all persons regardless of employments should act to His glory and honor.

Christian Citizenship

We reaffirm our commitment to bring the word of God, the mind of Christ, and the power of the Spirit to bear in developing moral courage, social sensitivity, and ethical responsibility as an inseparable part of Christian citizenship.

We further reaffirm that there is no dichotomy in Christian vocations—one God, one Lord, and one Christian calling.

Therefore, we reaffirm that the church not only has God's mandate in Christ to summon believers to service, but also has a mandate to provide training for responsible Christian leadership in every area of life.

Response and Follow-Up

In the early stages of planning, the leaders dared hope for an attendance of 500 at the National Colloquium. However, momentum continued to build up so that the total attendance reached over 900. In every way the venture may be regarded as highly successful. Immediately following the session, letters of commendation began arriving. As examples of the hearty endorsement of Baptist leaders, we quote several of these.

Congratulations on a job well done in the Colloquium on Christian Education!

Nashville, Tennessee

The meeting in Williamsburg was the best thing of its kind I have ever attended. It was a major contribution to education among Southern Baptists. I believe you moved us to a new plateau.

—Duke K. McCall, President
Southern Baptist Theological Seminary
Louisville, Kentucky

Thank you for this great experience. In my thirty years in the ministry this was the highlight in my many wonderful experiences in our denomination.

—R. Wilbur Herring
President
Arkansas Baptist State Convention
Little Rock, Arkansas

Congratulations on a splendid Colloquium on Christian Education. I felt it was a truly significant meeting, one with historical implications.

—R. G. Puckett
Editor, *The Maryland Baptist*
Lutherville, Maryland

The Colloquium was one of the finest things that I have ever attended.

—Dotson M. Nelson, Jr., Trustee,
Samford University, and First
Vice-President of the Southern
Baptist Convention
Birmingham, Alabama

Commendations and congratulations have come from leaders of several other denominations who are contemplating a similar conference for their schools.

In the words of Dr. Fisher, "The Colloquium is Prologue." Sensing that there is a need to be reminded that this significant project should not be considered as closed, and that in reality it should be but the beginning of intensive efforts on the part of Baptist colleges to implement the vision provided by this historic conference, a Follow-up Advisory Committee is already at work to insure an effective plan for conserving and vitalizing the benefits of the colloquium. This committee consists of the following men:

Herbert C. Gabhart, chairman; president, Belmont College, Nashville, Tennessee;
Grover J. Andrews, consultant; associate executive secretary, Commission on Colleges, Southern Association of Colleges and Schools, Atlanta, Georgia;
George E. Bagley, executive secretary-treasurer, Alabama State Convention, Montgomery, Alabama;
John A. Fincher, president emeritus, Carson-Newman College, Jefferson City, Tennessee;
E. Bruce Heilman, president, University of Richmond, Richmond, Virginia;
Ruric E. Wheeler, vice president for academic affairs, Samford University, Birmingham, Alabama;
Ex Officio
Ben C. Fisher, executive director-treasurer, Education Commission, Southern Baptist Convention;
George E. Capps, Jr., associate executive director, Education Commission, Southern Baptist Convention.

One extremely important development for higher education

among Southern Baptists has come out of the National Colloquium. Among the leaders in higher education in America who participated in this conference was Dr. Earl J. McGrath, senior adviser of the Lilly Endowment and executive director of the Program in Liberal Studies at the University of Arizona. Dr. McGrath has strong convictions on the value of church-related colleges in America, and the story of his contribution to the follow-up of the National Colloquium is told in the next chapter.

society laboring under a confusion of purpose, and regain for this generation of youth an appreciation of those transcendent eternal values which give enduring meaning to the human enterprise.

CHAPTER VIII

Even before the closing session of the National Colloquium, there was a strong conviction among Southern Baptist educators that many benefits, both direct and indirect, would be coming to Southern Baptist schools. However, none of the college presidents was aware of the fact that a significant, tangible development with far-reaching consequences was already at hand. This was a project from which all the colleges could benefit and which, because of an extremely generous grant, would cost these schools relatively little money.

In the early part of May, 1976, Dr. Ben C. Fisher, executive director-treasurer of the Education Commission, received an unexpected telephone call from Dr. Earl J. McGrath, senior adviser to the Lilly Endowment, and director of the Program in Liberal Studies at the University of Arizona. Dr. McGrath had accepted an invitation for a major speaking role at the National Colloquium of Southern Baptist Schools and Colleges, June 9-12, 1976, and while doing research for his address had become very much interested in what appeared to be the strength and commitment of Southern Baptist colleges and universities. He was especially attracted by the colloquium emphasis on values, a field of his own special interest and one on which he had produced several books and monographs.

He suggested that there would be possibly as much as $100,000 available, through the Program in Liberal Studies, for an exhaustive study of Southern Baptist colleges, provided that some matching funds could be produced by the Baptist educational institutions.

Dr. John A. Fincher, president of Carson-Newman College, was at this time president of the Association of Southern Baptist Colleges and Schools. Naturally Dr. Fisher took up the matter with him immediately, and Dr. Fincher appointed a Steering Committee consisting of:

E. Bruce Heilman, Chairman

Daniel R. Grant

Abner V. McCall

William G. Tanner

William K. Weaver, Jr.

After thorough discussion, this committee voted unanimously and enthusiastically to recommend that Southern Baptist colleges and universities participate in this study.

In making his proposal, Dr. McGrath stated: "I have for many years been concerned with the role of the church-related liberal arts college. I firmly believe that these institutions provide an essential element of strength and diversity in American education, and deserve greater attention and support than they now receive." These strong convictions of Dr. McGrath encouraged Southern Baptist college presidents to engage in this study.

Elaborating his stand, Dr. McGrath stated positively that he was interested in assisting Southern Baptist Colleges for the following reasons: their relative financial strength; their relative stability in enrollment; their willingness to wear without apology a church-related label; and their dedication to the transmission of values. Dr. McGrath believes that the verification of these strengths could be helpful to both public and private education.

Since the annual meeting of the Southern Baptist Convention was held in Norfolk, Virginia, immediately after the close of the National Colloquium in Williamsburg, Virginia, it was fitting for Dr. Fisher in his usual report to the Convention to announce plans for the prospective study. The response was instant, and the project received wide endorsement, particularly through editorials in the Baptist state papers.

Likewise the approval of Southern Baptist schools was prompt and enthusiastic. Within less than two weeks after this announcement, 49 of the 53 eligible Baptist educational institutions had agreed to participate in this study. These 49 schools were:

Averett College	Missouri Baptist College
Baptist College at Charleston	Mobile College

· East Texas Baptist College   Wake Forest University

East Texas Baptist College	Wake Forest University
Furman University	Wayland Baptist College
Gardner-Webb College	William Carey College
Georgetown College	William Jewell College
Grand Canyon College	Anderson College
Hardin-Simmons University	Bluefield College
Houston Baptist University	Brewton-Parker College
Judson College	Chowan College
Louisiana College	Clarke College
Mars Hill College	Hannibal-LaGrange College
Mary Hardin-Baylor College	North Greenville College
Mercer University	Southern Baptist College
Meredith College	Wingate College
Mississippi College	

As the project developed and materials accumulated, it became evident that this was to be the largest study of church-related colleges ever undertaken. Dr. McGrath and his associates Maurice Middleberg and Richard Neese estimated that they handled more than 45,000 pages of submitted data. This giant undertaking received considerable attention from Baptist state papers and Religious News Service. It is interesting to note, also, the interest in this study displayed by several other denominations.

Some readers may wonder just what were the primary objectives in this huge undertaking. To answer this, Dr. Fisher refers to the preface to Volume I of the McGrath report entitled *Study of Southern Baptist Colleges and Universities 1976-77,* first issued in July, 1977, and reprinted by the Education Commission in September of this year:

> . . . to determine the purposes of the constituent colleges and universities and to assess their present programs and activities in terms of their goals. To make such a review it was necessary, among other things, to obtain from each of the participating colleges a considerable body of information related to their goals, their religious commitments and activities, their financial condition, their governance, and their services to the communities of which they are a part.

The instruments used in making this study were the Church-College Relationship Questionnaire, the Institutional Functioning Inventory, the Inventory of Institutional Goals, and the Minter Financial Trends Questionnaire.

As the study progressed, there was constant communication between the McGrath team and the officials of the Education Commission since there were many points where questions needed to be answered and clarification made. Dr. George Capps, associate secretary of the Education Commission, gave much valuable help during the development and completion of the study.

More than 132 items were used to analyze and describe each of the 49 schools. In this process the opinions of many individual trustees, administrators, faculty, staff, alumni, and students were obtained by the McGrath team.

Of course general reports were made to the Education Commission offices, and also to the colleges. Each college received its individual report, which was done in code, with the key to the code furnished only to that school. In this way the report of each college was kept private.

The author has asked Dr. Fisher to give an interpretation of the results of this important study:

> While the findings of the McGrath report were overwhelmingly favorable, one of the greatest values

of the study is the frank way in which the research documents some obvious weaknesses which need to be corrected. Among the major weaknesses are the need to clarify statements of purpose; the need to have administration, faculty, trustees, and students reconcile their understanding of institutional goals; the need to reassess social concerns and community service

stituency support.

On the whole, Southern Baptist colleges and universities scored high on *esprit de corps,* innovation, commitment to teaching, stability in enrollment, financial stability, and fulfillment of purpose.

More importantly, the study indicates that the institutions that participated desire a close relationship to their Baptist constituency. Dr. McGrath states that these schools have maintained stronger church and denominational ties than any other body of schools in the nation. He also believes that this close church-relatedness has to be a factor in their general good health. This conclusion is further substantiated by John Minter in his financial analysis. Minter feels that the high rate of giving in support of current operations is directly attributable to Baptist schools' close ties to their denomination.

In addition, the McGrath *Study of Southern Baptist Colleges and Universities 1976-77* points out that in the past ten years private institutions all over the country have increased their enrollments by only about ten per cent, but during this same period Southern Baptist institutions have increased their enrollment by thirty-one per cent.

In commenting on the study, Dr. McGrath concluded with the following observations: "My associates and I have had long experience in examining institutions of higher learning. This group of Southern Baptist institutions is in about the best condition of any denominational group we have examined.

"There is nothing in our report that I would find really damaging—and that's most unusual for a study of this type. It is a most encouraging report to Baptists from an outsider," said McGrath, a layman of the United Presbyterian Church, U.S.A. He continued:

> I would hope that some of the positive practices so clearly exhibited by these testing scales would be retained and strengthened.
>
> The commitment of Southern Baptist academic communities to their churches, and to our kind of Judeo-Christian society—especially to the transmitting of moral values—should be confirmed by this year-long study and report.
>
> We hope our study leads to all kinds of reaction groups on individual campuses and in collective educational councils of the Southern Baptist family.
>
> This study will be of value to individual institutions only to the extent that they apply the findings seriously in planning their future development.
>
> The most glaring need revealed by the study is the urgent necessity for trustees, administration and faculty—and in some cases students—to fully understand the institution's basic purposes and for all to come to a meeting of the minds as to how to meet those purposes.

CHAPTER IX

In spite of rising costs and the many other troubles which have beset church-related higher education, since World War II Southern Baptist colleges and schools have been, in general, stronger than at any previous time in the history of the Southern Baptist Convention.

Colleges and Universities

While overall enrollments in church-related colleges during the past decade have tended to decrease, during this period the over-all enrollment in Southern Baptist colleges has increased by 31 percent.

Statistics from the years 1951 to 1971 are impressive. Enrollment increased from 55,460 to 120,456. Volumes in the libraries increased from 1,571,721 to 5,832,267. Total property value increased from $87,524,000 to $882,228,769. Of even greater significance is the fact that Baptist colleges since their founding have graduated almost 400,000 students.

Moreover, in an article called "Overview of Southern Baptist Higher Education," Ben C. Fisher documents the remarkable academic progress that Southern Baptist colleges had made up to the year 1971:

In summary, it may be said that the period 1951 to 1971 was an era of academic progress for Southern Baptist colleges and universities. Developments included accreditation of all 53 institutions by regional accrediting agencies; a change from strict liberal arts emphasis to liberal arts orientation with provision for vocational and professional education as well, and relaxation of rigid academic divisions in favor of team-teaching, interdisciplinary courses, and independent study; vastly improved library holdings, staff, and facilities; growing use of interinstitutional cooperation for curriculum enrichment, resource-sharing, and community service; notable progress in faculty-student participation in governance; increasing acceptance of responsibility for continuing education of adults; a growing consciousness of the need to develop stronger programs to assist faculty members in professional improvement; and the development of a variety of substantive foreign study programs for students.

The McGrath study, described in the preceding chapter, in most respects substantiates these findings and indicates that there continue to be many areas of progress among Southern Baptist colleges. From three major studies, all undertaken within the last ten years (the *Baptist Education Study Task* in 1967, "Overview of Southern Baptist Higher Education" in 1971, and the *Study of Southern Baptist Colleges and Universities 1976-77*), several reasons may be listed for the relative good health of Southern Baptist educational institutions: a concern for Christian purpose and a desire to serve the denomination; employment practices (in seeking both faculty and administrative officers) that give preference to Christian commitment; curricula that reflect special emphasis on Christian vocations and teaching of the Bible; teaching-centered rather than research-centered academic goals; commitment to high academic standards; determination to hold the line on Christian moral values and conduct; sound fiscal management; aggressive student recruitment; realistic long-range planning; strong, committed, and aggressive administrators; and new and more effective methods of trustee orientation.

94

In addition to the substantial progress made by Southern Baptist colleges and universities during the past twenty-five years, there are other causes for optimism. Dr. Earl J. McGrath and Richard C. Neese in their recent excellent paper entitled "Are the Church-Related Colleges Losing Students?"* feel that pessimism regarding the enrollment at church-related colleges is not justified:

Furthermore, other national church-related groups have conducted in-depth studies of their colleges and have pledged to renew support for these institutions. Recent major studies have been made by the National Catholic Education Association, the Lutheran Educational Conference of America, and the Board of Higher Education and Ministry of the United Methodist Church. The report on the latter study begins with this significant statement: "The United Methodist Church, continuing its 200-year history, is in higher education to stay." Thus there seems to be a genuinely favorable shift in the direction of renewed support for the church-related college. This opinion is shared by such well-known Christian educators as Elton Trueblood, Earl J. McGrath, Gerald Kennedy, Abner V. McCall, and Michael Blecker. All of these agree, however, that continuation of support will be predicated upon willingness of the colleges to wear their church-related label without apology. Southern Baptist colleges and schools, in adopting the "Reaffirmations" at Williamsburg, stated clearly and unmistakably that they intend to remain church-related institutions, actively supporting the work of the churches and the denomination. If they succeed in this intent, their future seems assured.

---

* First published by the Program in Liberal Studies at the University of Arizona in November, 1976, and reprinted in full in *The Southern Baptist Educator,* March-April, 1977.

Seminaries

In order to assess properly the future of Southern Baptist theological education, some understanding is needed of past performance. Southern Baptist theological seminaries have experienced a remarkable growth, and unquestionably these institutions, almost entirely supported through the Cooperative Program of the Southern Baptist Convention, will continue to play an extremely vital role in the future development of the churches and all other agencies and institutions of the Convention. Just as in the case of the colleges, the statistics are impressive. In the period from 1951 to 1971, Southern Baptist theological seminaries showed great progress. Total enrollments increased from 4,574 in 1951 to 16,566 in 1971. During the same period the number of volumes in the libraries increased from 166,028 to 855,883, while property value increased from $18,107,000 to $86,880,991. More than 35,000 students have graduated from these institutions.

A quotation from the "Overview of Southern Baptist Higher Education" will explain current developments which have been formative in the growth of the seminaries:

> The growing need for professionally educated vocational Christian workers has had a profound influence on the development of curriculum and educational objectives in the seminaries. In 1951 there were approximately 2,800 students in Southern Baptist theological schools who were preparing at the B.D. level for the pastorate. Only 666 were listed as preparing for other Christian vocations. Because of the manner of reporting, the figure 666 may be low, but it is doubtful whether the number in any case exceeded 750. However, by 1971 there were enrolled at the seminary undergraduate level 3,563 ministerial students and 2,102 students preparing for other Christian vocations. Currently there are between 37 and 40 percent of the students in Southern Baptist theological seminaries at the M.Div. (or B.D.) level who are preparing for Christian vocations other than that of the pastoral ministry.

This diversification of ministries has resulted in the development of three major academic thrusts: in theology, religious education, and music. To be sure, the structure of these programs varies from seminary to seminary, but whether they are defined as schools, departments, or areas of study, these are the three divisions which have become the basis for curriculum development. In several seminaries, these divisions

of Theological Schools and accreditation the six seminaries by the national accrediting agencies of their regions. The latter agencies are responsible for accreditation of all higher education, public and private. Some of the accreditation of Southern Baptist seminaries had been accomplished prior to 1951, but it has been within the last twenty years that the standards of accrediting agencies have made more strenuous demands.

In recent years a significant change has been made in seminary degree programs. Southern Baptist theological institutions, in keeping with the national trends, now offer the Master of Divinity degree (M.Div.) instead of the Bachelor of Divinity (B.D.).

There has also been a marked improvement in the academic preparation of the faculties. A substantial number of faculty members now hold degrees from, or have done post-doctoral work in, outstanding colleges and universities both at home and abroad. Included in these schools are such universities as Basel, Cambridge, Heidelberg, London, Oxford, Paris, Tübingen, Zürich, etc., in Europe, and the University of Chicago, Harvard, Princeton, Union Theological Seminary, and Yale.

One of the more promising developments has been the growth and service of the Seminary Extension Department, a joint project of the six Southern Baptist theological seminaries. Dr. Raymond M.

Rigdon, director of the Seminary Extension Department, lists the following significant developments during the 1970s: development of three curriculum series, graded by levels of difficulty, which provide viable continuing education opportunities for all pastors regardless of limitations or extent of previous educational experiences; establishment of Home Study Institute and its accreditation by the Accrediting Commission of the National Home Study Council; and induction into membership of the National University Extension Association.

Bible Schools

The contribution of the Baptist Bible schools for some time, perhaps, has not been properly recognized. These institutions grew out of the very desperate need of a large number of ministers who had only a high school education or less, but who were highly motivated and willing to serve in the poorest areas of the convention, many times with little pay. According to a "Study of the Educational Attainment of Southern Baptist Pastors" produced jointly by the Home Mission Board and the Education Commission and published in 1973, approximately thirty-five percent of Southern Baptist pastors still had at that time only a high school education or less, and only about forty-seven percent had both college and seminary training. There are currently four Bible schools supported by the churches of the states in which they are located: Baptist Bible Institute in Lakeland, Florida; Clear Creek Baptist School, Clear Creek, Kentucky; Fruitland Baptist Institute, Hendersonville, North Carolina; and Mexican Bible Institute, San Antonio, Texas. There is a fifth Bible school, primarily for black students, the American Baptist Theological Seminary in Nashville, Tennessee, which is supported jointly by the Southern and National Baptist Convention, U.S.A., Incorporated. These schools have an enrollment of approximately 2000, and all serve very effectively a Baptist constituency far beyond these states in which they are located.

In the beginning, several of these institutions came into being as a result of the interest of one founder, and for many years continued on a very informal and loosely organized basis, with most courses concentrated in Biblical areas and some attention to homiletics. In the latter years, there has been an enormous improvement in faculties, facilities, and curriculum, and these institutions are now engaged in the truest sense in broad programs of adult education. In several schools the quality of work is such that both Southern Baptist colleges and seminaries are now giving credit for this work.

Academies

Southern Baptists still support seven Baptist academies. These include Fork Union Military Academy, Fork Union, Virginia;

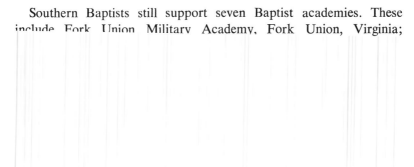

education in one of these institutes. These include such men as the late Dr. George Truett, and Dr. William F. Powell, for many years pastor of the First Baptist Church in Nashville, Tennessee. Approximately 3,000 students are currently enrolled in the academies, which continue to render an outstanding service to Southern Baptists.

Conclusion

The story of the growth of the Southern Baptist Convention from a small handful of followers led by Shubal Stearns more than two hundred years ago to the largest Protestant denomination in the country cannot be separated from the history of its colleges, universities, seminaries, Bible schools, and academies.

Baptist schools have restated their commitment to their Christian purpose, clearly outlined in the Williamsburg colloquium reaffirmations. Baptist leaders and people have never been more solidly behind their educational institutions. The future seems bright for both the churches and their schools.

Appendix

STUDIES AND PAPERS ON BAPTIST AND OTHER
CHURCH-RELATED HIGHER EDUCATION

by the Council on the Church Related ...

nessee: General Board of Education, The United Methodist
Church, 1971.

Boren, David L. "The Recovery of Integrity in Citizenship," *Southern Baptist Educator,* Vol. XLI, No. 2 (November-December, 1976), 6-10.

Bornley, Jesse P. *Two Centuries of Methodist Concern: Bondage, Freedom, and Education of Black People.* New York: Vintage Press, 1974.

Chafin, Kenneth. "Baptist Schools and a Covenant Relationship," *Southern Baptist Educator,* Vol. XL, No. 6 (July-August, 1976), 14-16.

Challenges of Change to the Christian College. Proceedings of the Fourth Quadrennial Convocation of Christian Colleges, June 19-23, 1966, Earlham College, Richmond, Indiana. Washington, D.C.: Council of Protestant Colleges and Universities, 1966.

A College-Related Church. United Methodist Perspectives. Nashville, Tennessee: National Commission on United Methodist Higher Education, 1976.

Connors, Manning Austin, Jr. *Curricular Change and Innovation in Selected Church-Related Institutions of Higher Education 1961-1970.* Submitted in partial fulfillment of the requirements for the Doctor of Education degree in the School of Education, Indiana University, June, 1971.

Cothen, Grady C. *Faith and Higher Education.* 1975 Hester Lecture Series. Nashville, Tennessee: Broadman Press, 1976.

Endangered Service. Independent Colleges, Public Policy and the First Amendment. Nashville, Tennessee: National Commission on United Methodist Higher Education, 1976.

Fisher, Ben C. "Catholic College Presidents and Bishops Explore Ways to Collaborate" (editorial), *Southern Baptist Educator,* Vol. XLI, No. 4 (March-April, 1977), 13.

Fisher, Ben C. *An Orientation Manual for College Trustees.* Third edition, revised. Nashville, Tennessee: Education Commission, Southern Baptist Convention, 1971.

Fisher, Ben C. "Overview of Southern Baptist Higher Education 1951-1971," *Southern Baptist Educator,* Vol. XXXVIII, No. 2 (November-December, 1973), 3-13.

Fisher, Ben C. "Preliminary Outline for Developing Colloquium and Three-Year Follow-up Period," Background Papers, National Colloquium on Christian Education, June 9-12, 1976, Williamsburg, Virginia, *Southern Baptist Educator* (Special edition, June, 1976), 2-7.

Fisher, Ben C., ed. "A Statement of the Aims and Objectives of Christian Higher Education." A study prepared by the Council on Christian Education of the Baptist State Convention of North Carolina, October, 1965.

Ford, LeRoy. "Continuing Education of Church and Denominational Leaders." A study prepared for the Academic Education Subcommittee of the Inter-Agency Council of the Southern Baptist Convention, Nashville, Tennessee, 1968. (Mimeographed)

Geer, William D. "Fringe Benefits in Southern Baptist Colleges 1972-73." Birmingham, Alabama: Samford University, 1972. (Mimeographed)

Grant, Daniel R. "The Significance of the McGrath Study of 49 Southern Baptist Colleges and Universities: Seeing Ourselves as Others See Us," *Southern Baptist Educator,* Vol. XLI, No. 6 (July-August, 1977), 5-6, 15.

Harris, Fred E. "Reexamining the Christian View of the Student-Teacher Relationship," *Southern Baptist Educator,* Vol. XLI, No. 2 (November-December, 1976), 4-5.

Hester, H. I. *The Christian College.* Nashville, Tennessee: The Sunday School Board, Southern Baptist Convention, 1940.

Hester, H. I. *Partners in Purpose and Progress: A Brief History of the Education Commission of the Southern Baptist Convention.* Nashville, Tennessee: Education Commission of the Southern Baptist Convention, 1977.

Hester, H. I. *Southern Baptists in Christian Education.* Murfrees-

Institutional History 1826-1954). Waco, Texas. The Baylor University Press, 1955.

Jones, Edward N., ed. "The Future Development of the Christian Education Program of the Baptist General Convention of Texas." A report prepared by the Christian Education Commission and the Ministerial and Study Committee, November 14, 1963.

La Bouve, Michael Frank. *A Study of Undergraduate Student Recruiting Programs in Southern Baptist Colleges and Universities.* A dissertation submitted to the Department of Higher Education in partial fulfillment of the requirements for the degree of Doctor of Philosophy, College of Education, Florida State University, June, 1971.

McBeth, Leon. *The History of Southern Baptist Higher Education.* Nashville, Tennessee: Education Commission of the Southern Baptist Convention, 1966.

McCall, Duke K. "The Baptist Role in Universal Higher Education." An address before the first national Baptist Education Study Task conference, Nashville, Tennessee, June 16, 1966.

McGrath, Earl J. *General Education and the Plight of Modern Man.* Indianapolis, Indiana: The Lilly Endowment, Inc., [n. d.].

McGrath, Earl J. *Study of Southern Baptist Colleges and Universities 1976-77.* Nashville, Tennessee: Education Commission of the Southern Baptist Convention, 1977.

McGrath, Earl J., and Richard C. Neese. *Are Church-Related Colleges Losing Students?* Higher Education Program Topical Paper Series 1976-77, No. 6. Tucson, Arizona: University of Arizona Press, 1977.

Moots, Philip R. "Pressing Legal Issues Confronting Church-Related Colleges." Address to the Association of Southern Baptist Colleges and Schools, June 29, 1977. *Southern Baptist Educator,* Vol. XLI, No. 6 (July-August, 1977), 9-12.

Newport, John P. "Presenting an Authentic Christian Witness in a World of Secularism and Religious Obsession, *Southern Baptist Educator,* Vol. XLI, No. 2 (November-December, 1976), 11-17.

Pattillo, Manning M., Jr. "Implications of the Danforth Study of Church-Related Colleges for Southern Baptists." An address before the first national Baptist Education Study Task conference, Nashville, Tennessee, June 14, 1966.

"Reaffirmations." Adopted by Association of Southern Baptist Colleges and Schools, Williamsburg, Virginia. *Southern Baptist Educator,* Vol. XL, No. 6 (July-August, 1976), 1, 24.

Religious Education Courses Offered in Southern Baptist Colleges. Lewis Wingo, Project Analyst. Nashville, Tennessee: Sunday School Board of the Southern Baptist Convention (Church Services and Materials Division), March, 1973.

Report of the Committee of 20 to Baptist State Convention of North Carolina. Annual Session, November 10-12, 1969, Fayetteville, North Carolina.

Review and Expositor. "The Church and the University." Summer issue, 1972. Vol. LXIX, No. 3.

Robb, Felix C. "If I Were a Baptist." A paper presented at the annual meeting of the Association of Southern Baptist Colleges and Schools, Furman University, Greenville, South Carolina, June 19, 1968.

Smiley, David L. "Redeeming the Christian Idea of the Liberal Education," Background Papers, National Colloquium on Christian Education, June 9-12, 1976, Williamsburg, Virginia, *Southern Baptist Educator* (Special edition, June, 1976), 21-27.

Smith, H. B. "Patterns of Decision-Making Involving Administration and Faculty." A paper presented at the annual meeting of the Association of Southern Baptist Colleges and Schools, Furman University, Greenville, South Carolina, June 19, 1968.

Spinks, W. Robert. *Interinstitutional Cooperation Among the Colleges and Universities of the Southern Baptist Convention: A Survey and Proposal.* Submitted in partial fulfillment of the requirements for

Report to the Joint Committee of the Division for Mission in North America and the Council of Lutheran Church in America Colleges, prepared by Merton P. Strommen, assisted by Shelby Andress, Youth Research Center. Minneapolis, Minnesota: Division for Mission in North America, Lutheran Church in America, 1976.

Tanner, William G. "Partners in Purpose and Progress," *Southern Baptist Educator,* Vol. XLI, No. 2 (November-December, 1976), 18-21.

Trueblood, Elton. "The Redemption of the College," *Southern Baptist Educator,* Vol. XL, No. 6 (July-August, 1976), 8-13.

Wilson, Edwin. "The Primacy of Teaching in the Next Century," Background Papers, National Colloquium on Christian Education, June 9-12, 1976, Williamsburg, Virginia, *Southern Baptist Educator* (Special edition, June, 1976), 15-20.

Wilson, Edwin G. "Student Participation in Institutional Affairs." A paper presented at the annual meeting of the Association of Southern Baptist Colleges and Schools, Furman University, Greenville, South Carolina, June 19, 1968.

105

PROGRAM STATEMENT OF EDUCATION COMMISSION

Purpose—

The purpose of the Education Commission is to promote cooperation between the educational institutions officially sponsored by the state Baptist Conventions and/or Baptist district associations and the agencies of the Southern Baptist Convention, to provide specific services to Baptist colleges and schools, and to maintain liaison for them with the regional accrediting associations, the United States Office of Education, state boards of higher education, boards of higher education in other religious bodies, and professional educational organizations and learned societies.

The Education Commission reflects Southern Baptist commitment to introduce Christian truth into every area of life and to be obedient to the clear intent of the Scriptures in carrying out a teaching ministry. This teaching ministry is accomplished through a system of seminaries, universities, colleges, academies, and Bible schools which constitute the Southern Baptist educational enterprise.

Functions—

1. Christian education leadership and coordination—Coordinates service programs between state Baptist schools, SBC agencies and programs, and state conventions when such coordination is mutually helpful.

2. College studies and services—Cooperates with the colleges and their officers in providing studies and services for improving performance in such areas as denominational relations, finances, curriculum, management, public relations, recruitment of students, and publishes a Southern Baptist educational journal for administrators, faculty members, trustees, and Baptist leaders.

3. Teacher-personnel placement services—Provides a registry for Baptist college teachers and administrative personnel who have superior academic qualifications, are active churchmen, and who are in complete sympathy with the purposes of a Baptist college.

4. Student recruitment—Assists Baptist colleges in developing an effective program of student recruitment and prepares materials informing Baptist high school students of the opportunities available to them in Southern Baptist colleges.

5. Convention relations—Works with colleges and state conventions to secure better convention-college relationships through Baptist state papers, workshops, seminars, and national conferences.

Relationships—

Cooperates with Seminary Extension Department to make better use of Seminary Extension materials, utilizing district associations, college personnel and facilities in the training of ministers and others seeking help at professional levels. Works with the program of National Student Ministries to improve communications between the Baptist student ministry and the colleges. Works with the program of Church Administration Services to help relate the choice of vocations to the choice of colleges. Works with the regional and national accrediting associations, the United States Office of Education, state boards of higher education, and boards of other religious bodies, in order to interpret and alert the colleges to trends and policies affecting them.

Reporting—

(1) Annual statistical report on the schools, (2) highlights of the program in the Convention *Annual* and *Book of Reports,* (3) long-range objectives, annual goals and goal achievement in the Convention Budget and Financial Data procedures.

Adopted by the Southern Baptist Convention June 6, 1972.

108

PAST PRESIDENTS OF THE ASSOCIATION
OF SOUTHERN BAPTIST COLLEGES AND SCHOOLS

1948-49 Walter Pope Binns

1956-57 George B. Connell
1957-58 J. I. Riddle
1958-59 H. Leo Eddleman
1959-60 Charles L. Harman
1960-61 Evan A. Reiff
1961-62 James M. Boswell
1962-63 J. Ralph Noonkester
1963-64 D. Harley Fite
1964-65 Curtis L. Bishop
1965-66 Robert L. Mills
1966-67 Herbert C. Gabhart
1967-68 Bruce E. Whitaker
1968-69 Leslie S. Wright
1969-70 James Ralph Scales
1970-71 G. Earl Guinn
1971-72 Gordon W. Blackwell
1972-73 W. Lewis Nobles
1973-74 Abner V. McCall
1974-75 James L. Sells
1975-76 John A. Fincher
1976-77 E. Bruce Heilman
1977-78 William K. Weaver, Jr.

STATISTICAL INFORMATION ON SOUTHERN BAPTIST COLLEGES, SEMINARIES, AND SCHOOLS

SENIOR COLLEGES AND UNIVERSITIES—1976-1977

NAME	LOCATION	PRESIDENT	Faculty Including Administrative Officers	Enrollment Fall 1976 Reg.	Enrollment Fall 1976 Total	Enrollment Total 1976-1977 Reg.	Enrollment Total 1976-1977 Total	Graduate Students Enrolled	Graduated Sept. 1975-Aug. 1976	Graduated Since Founding	Ministry Students Pastoral	Ministry Students Educational	Ministry Students Music	Vacations Students Other Church	Total Church Vacations Volunteers	Home and Foreign Mission Volunteers	Volumes in Library Excluding Public Documents
Averett College	Danville, Virginia	Conwell A. Anderson	54	1,063	1,063	1,249	1,249		239	5,465	25	18	3	10	56	5	53,874
Baptist Col. at Charleston	Charleston, S.C.	John A. Hamrick	84	2,290	2,290	6,592	6,592		328	2,582	67	36	37	188	328	213	89,271
Baylor University	Waco, Texas	Abner V. McCall	437	9,057	9,057	13,325	13,325	836	2,055	54,832	324	240	159	489	1,212	194	786,885
Belmont College	Nashville, Tenn.	Herbert C. Gabhart	84	1,160	1,160	1,500	1,500		265	2,645	41	41	40	10	96	9	68,390
Bluefield College	Bluefield, Va.	Charles L. Tyer	30	350	350	441	441		65	3,423	25	13	12		50		41,000
Blue Mountain College [2]	Blue Mountain, Mississippi	E. Harold Fisher	36	285	285	452	490		57	3,885	5		21		123	3	41,087
California Baptist College	Riverside, California	James R. Staples	45	822	822	985	985		135	1,660	122	76	123	14	417	20	96,000
Campbell College	Buie's Creek, N.C.	Norman A. Wiggins	104	2,077	2,077	2,518	2,820	97	394	13,027	91	42	6	96	178	71	135,766
Campbellsville College	Campbellsville, Ky.	William R. Davenport	62	686	686	867	867		135	2,216	95	9	32	52	219	6	78,000
Carson-Newman College	Jefferson City, Tenn.	John A. Fincher	108	1,695	1,695	2,089	2,874		345	9,952	157	27	30	65	187	26	127,101
Cumberland College	Williamsburg, Ky.	J. M. Boswell	101	1,879	1,879	2,728	2,808		312	9,981	394	35	17	45	254	40	74,000
Dallas Baptist College	Dallas, Texas	W. E. Thorn	76	1,228	1,228	1,556	1,556		281	1,519	177	19	75	41	525	46	154,630
East Texas Baptist College	Marshall, Texas	Jerry F. Dawson	54	793	793	999	1,012		79	2,724	177	21	56	41	295	7	84,000
Furman University	Greenville, S.C.	John E. Johns	168	2,721	3,046	3,521	4,953	412	565	16,029	75	39	42	49	219	26	227,084
Gardner-Webb College	Boiling Springs, N.C.	Craven Edward Williams	100	1,354	1,368	1,875	1,893		538	5,571	166	76	53	10	294	20	86,789
Georgetown College	Georgetown, Ky.	Robert L. Mills	83	1,020	1,020	1,098	1,098		212	8,338	27	6	19	11	97	13	120,811
Grand Canyon College	Phoenix, Arizona	William R. Hinze	46	1,134	1,137	1,655	1,662	53	202	1,969	156	15	20	19	200	20	71,619
Hannibal-LaGrange College	Hannibal, Missouri	Gerald Martin	28	355	469	568	587		91	4,160	62	6	21	25	122	13	25,000
Hardin-Simmons Univ.	Abilene, Texas	Elwin L. Skiles	102	1,717	1,717	2,577	2,577	280	262	12,752	152	32	59	24	141	11	141,450
Houston Baptist Univ.	Houston, Texas	William H. Hinton	96	1,693	1,693	2,502	2,502		170	1,330	150	9	38	29	226	24	95,161
Howard Payne Univ.	Brownwood, Texas	Roger L. Brooks	93	1,475	1,592	2,043	2,296		245	8,929	256	30	7	385	678	30	109,251
Judson College [2]	Marion, Alabama	N. H. McCrummen	37	372	372	428	465		72	3,807		8	18	67	93	8	50,304
Louisiana College	Pineville, Louisiana	Robert L. Lynn	74	1,279	1,316	1,842	1,903		154	5,751	132	74	70		276	31	89,000
Mars Hill College	Mars Hill, N.C.	Fred B. Bentley	133	1,756	1,756	2,355	2,355		379	10,813	30	8	50	28	122	13	100,000
Mary Hardin-Baylor College	Belton, Texas	Bobby E. Parker	84	1,116	1,116	1,670	1,670		239	5,929	17	4	11	4	36	2	107,155
Mercer University	Macon, Georgia	Rufus Carrollton Harris	200	3,615	3,615	4,390	5,005	79	788	7,351	52	4	5	10	109	8	180,000
Meredith College [2]	Raleigh, N.C.	John E. Weems	145	1,300	1,300	1,329	1,329		321	7,521		17	47	43	172	23	78,000
Mississippi College	Clinton, Mississippi	W. Lewis Nobles	145	3,051	3,200	3,958	4,077	1,696	765	15,915	59	22	39	52	172	10	154,260
Missouri Baptist College [1]	St. Louis, Missouri	Robert S. Sutherland	23	410	416	523	548		45	147				60	60		30,000
Mobile College	Mobile, Alabama	William K. Weaver, Jr.	67	903	919	1,144	1,155		196	1,000	148	25	35	7	192	10	54,047
Oklahoma Baptist Univ.	Shawnee, Oklahoma	William E. Neptune, Actg.	155	1,723	1,723	2,453	2,453		343	7,490	385	49	108	11	529	144	110,000
Ouachita Baptist Univ.	Arkadelphia, Arkansas	Daniel R. Grant	109	1,633	1,633	2,059	2,059	119	376	7,996	122	18	77	40	288	31	110,995
Palm Beach Atlantic College	W. Palm Beach, Florida	Warner Earle Fusselle	42	442	442	560	560		69	337	55	12	12	15	100	10	40,000
Richmond, Univ. of	Richmond, Virginia	E. Bruce Heilman	228	4,052	5,256	5,623	9,117	1,060	818	20,679	20	10	18	20	60	5	299,327
Samford Univ.	Birmingham, Alabama	Leslie S. Wright	199	3,846	6,993	5,424	9,158	1,480	879	17,017	38	30	125	160	655	32	215,696
Shorter College	Rome, Georgia	Randall H. Minor	68	843	843	957	1,718		83	17,691	4	4	58	124	124	12	73,300
Southwest Baptist College	Bolivar, Missouri	James L. Sells	83	1,443	1,443	1,718	1,718		220	2,041	370	42	91	129	632	69	64,710
Stetson Univ.	DeLand, Florida	Pope A. Duncan	150	2,898	2,949	3,351	3,485	230	624	14,984	65		24	10	99		278,374
Tift College [2]	Forsyth, Georgia	Robert W. Craig	37	702	702	845	845		95	4,109		6	4	4	14	3	52,000
Union Univ.	Jackson, Tenn.	Robert E. Craig	69	1,037	1,163	1,411	1,631		198	12,370	110	14	44	36	204	18	60,000
Virginia Intermont College [2]	Bristol, Virginia	Floyd V. Turner	50	644	644	759	759		142	6,864							54,500
Wake Forest Univ.	Winston-Salem, N.C.	James Ralph Scales	639	4,516	4,516	5,132	5,572	1,344	1,056	23,844	30	30	16	13	89	4	642,611
Wayland Baptist College	Plainview, Texas	Roy C. McClung	73	1,111					226	7,300	93	15	30		138	26	73,300
William Carey College	Hattiesburg, Miss.	J. Ralph Noonkester	103	1,526	2,042	2,247	2,973	935	447	4,502	107	33	82	8	230	26	88,115
William Jewell College	Liberty, Missouri	Thomas S. Field	106	1,616	1,616	2,097	2,097		282	7,724	107	33	82	100	100	10	122,504
Totals—Senior Colleges			4,944	76,874	83,280	105,817	119,363	8,621	15,744	375,337	4,905	1,188	1,849	2,503	10,445	1,308	5,832,267

[1] Candidate for full membership in regional accrediting association and approved by the State Department of Education; all other schools accredited by regional accrediting association

[2] Colleges for women

JUNIOR COLLEGES—1

NAME	LOCATION	PRESIDENT	Faculty, Including Administrative Officers	Enrollment Fall, 1976		Enrollment Total 1976-1977		Music Ministry Students	Other Church Vocations Students	Total Church Vocations Volunteers	Home and Foreign Mission Volunteers	Volumes in Library Excluding Public Documents
				Reg.	Total	Reg.	Tota					
Anderson College [1]	Anderson, S.C.	J. Cordell Maddox	55	1,203	1,203	1,481	1,53	12		29		22,985
Brewton-Parker College	Mount Vernon, Georgia	J. Theodore Phillips	41	555	555	930	93	5		32		17,630
Chowan College	Murfreesboro, N.C.	Bruce E. Whitaker	72	1,059	1,060	1,352	1,35	5	1	15	1	55,125
Clarke College	Newton, Mississippi	S. L. Harris	16	181	185	245	25	25		89		18,929
North Greenville College	Tigerville, S.C.	George Silver	39	558	609	902	96	30	12	73	4	32,875
Southern Baptist College	Walnut Ridge, Arkansas	D. Jack Nicholas	23	514	555	803	83	10	15	95	2	37,824
Truett-McConnell College	Cleveland, Georgia	Ronald E. Weitman	57	696	701	2,474	2,47	5		43	2	17,322
Wingate College	Wingate, N.C.	Thomas E. Corts	85	1,255	1,330	1,586	1,65	8		34	2	69,500
Totals—Junior Colleges			388	6,021	6,198	9,773	9,95	95	28	410	13	272,190

[1] All schools accredited by regional association.

SEMINARIES, ACADEMIES, BIBLE SCHOOLS—1976-1977

NAME	LOCATION	PRESIDENT	Faculty, Including Administrative Officers	Enrollment Fall 1976 Reg.	Enrollment Fall 1976 Total	Enrollment Total 1976-1977 Reg.	Enrollment Total 1976-1977 Total	Graduate Students Enrolled	Graduated Sept. 1975-Aug. 1976	Graduated Since Founding	Pastoral Ministry Students	Educational Ministry Students	Music Ministry Students	Other Church Vocations Students	Total Church Vocations Volunteers	Home and Foreign Mission Volunteers	Volumes in Library Excluding Public Documents
Seminaries																	
Golden Gate Baptist Theological Seminary [1,2]	Mill Valley, California	Harold K. Graves	39	396	438	479	550	357	71	1,581	313	74	33	59	479	22	89,500
Midwestern Baptist Theological Seminary [1,2]	Kansas City, Missouri	Milton Ferguson	30	356	450	623	631	397	79	906	269	52	4	34	359	39	68,006
New Orleans Baptist Theological Seminary [1,2]	New Orleans, Louisiana	Landrum P. Leavell	59	906	906	1,374	1,374	1,168	228	6,579	857	346	87	84	1,374	149	138,000
Southeastern Baptist Theological Seminary [1,2]	Wake Forest, N.C.	W. Randall Lolley	44	997	997	1,155	1,155	126	191	3,303	876	90	…	40	1,006	45	113,700
Southern Baptist Theological Seminary [1,2]	Louisville, Kentucky	Duke K. McCall	91	1,960	2,124	2,400	2,639	1,970	394	12,928	1,364	417	333	…	2,114	127	232,680
Southwestern Baptist Theological Seminary [1,2]	Fort Worth, Texas	Robert E. Naylor	118	3,202	3,202	3,851	3,851	3,583	616	15,967	2,246	1,221	384	…	3,851	425	213,197
Seminary Extension Department, S.B.C.					8,449		8,449										
Totals—Seminaries			381	7,817	16,566	9,882	18,649	7,601	1,579	41,264	5,925	2,200	841	217	9,183	807	855,083
Academies																	
Fork Union Military Academy [1]	Fork Union, Virginia	Kenneth T. Whitescarver	58	581	581	660	660	…	144	5,619	…	…	…	…	…	…	11,000
Hargrave Military Academy [1]	Chatham, Virginia	Vernon T. Lankford	35	257	257	357	357	…	51	3,395	…	…	…	…	…	…	15,012
Harrison-Chilhowee Baptist Academy [1]	Seymour, Tennessee	Hubert B. Smothers	18	158	158	297	297	…	37	2,005	…	…	2	…	11	4	6,150
Oak Hill Academy [3]	Mouth of Wilson, Va.	Robert B. Isner	22	191	191	350	350	…	50	1,879	9	…	…	…	…	…	4,400
Oneida Baptist Institute [3]	Oneida, Kentucky	Barkley Moore	30	335	335	335	335	…	34	1,843	…	…	…	…	…	…	10,000
San Marcos Baptist Academy [1]	San Marcos, Texas	Jack E. Byrom	40	382	382	442	664	…	79	3,302	…	…	…	…	…	…	12,950
Valley Baptist Academy [6]	Harlingen, Texas	H. E. Gary	12	180	180	188	188	…	21	307	10	…	…	…	10	…	5,000
Totals—Academies			215	2,084	2,084	2,629	2,851	…	416	18,350	19	…	2	…	21	4	64,512
Bible Schools																	
American Baptist College (American Bapt. Theol. Seminary) [4,5]	Nashville, Tennessee	Charles E. Boddie	15	100	779	152	706	…	23	553	80	13	…	58	151	1	14,500
Baptist Bible Institute [3]	Graceville, Florida	Joseph P. DuBose, Jr.	16	341	341	380	412	…	95	886	282	49	81	…	412	4	25,850
Clear Creek Baptist School	Pineville, Kentucky	D. M. Aldridge	11	254	254	269	269	…	54	725	160	…	4	…	164	2	9,000
Fruitland Baptist Bible Institute	Hendersonville, N.C.	Alex L. Booth, Jr.	12	224	224	214	214	…	83	978	214	…	…	…	214	…	11,500
Mexican Baptist Bible Institute	San Antonio, Texas	Daniel J. Rivera	11	83	83	125	125	…	21	181	47	40	1	3	91	86	11,000
Totals—Bible Schools			65	1,002	1,681	1,140	1,726	…	276	3,323	783	102	86	61	1,032	93	71,850

[1] Accreditation by regional association
[2] Member, Association of Theological Schools, on accredited list
[3] Accreditation by state department of education (or state university)
[4] Supported jointly with National Baptist Convention, U.S.A., Incorporated
[5] Member, Council on Postsecondary Accreditation
[6] Figures used are for 1975-1976